T0149970

The Army and Multinational Force Compatibility

Michele Zanini · Jennifer Morrison Taw

Arroyo Center

RAND

Prepared for the United States Army

For more information on the RAND Arroyo Center, contact the Director of Operations, (310) 393-0411, extension 6500, or visit the Arroyo Center's Web site at http://www.rand.org/organization/ard/

This publication presents the results of work done for the Office of the Deputy Under Secretary of the Army for International Affairs (DUSA-IA) in FY98 anticipating the potential effects of Force XXI on multinational force compatibility in future coalition operations. This work was done in conjunction with a study examining the implications of land force dominance for U.S. Army engagement, sponsored by the Office of the U.S. Army Deputy Chief of Staff for Intelligence (DCSINT).

Both studies were undertaken within RAND Arroyo Center's Strategy, Doctrine, and Resources Program. The Arroyo Center is a federally funded research and development center sponsored by the United States Army. This work should be of interest to Army planners, as well as to students of multinational military operations and to the broader defense community.

CONTENTS

TABLES

SUMMARY

As part of its Force XXI development program, the U.S. Army is "digitizing" the force: interweaving its various levels of command with sophisticated information technologies to provide a clear and accurate shared picture of the battlespace, or area of operations, at all levels, from the commander down to the individual soldier. The intention is to increase dramatically the scope and quality of shared situational awareness, to permit units to synchronize and resynchronize operations smoothly and quickly, and to be able to focus fires, logistics, and other resources wherever they are needed, without being rigidly limited by traditional organizational boundaries.

In turn, improved situational awareness should enable standoff, nonlinear, dispersed operations, as opposed to the more conventional approach of massing forces to conduct close combat on a clearly delineated battlefield. The Force XXI process is also expected to facilitate enhanced force protection, leaner logistics, and split-based operations.

The Army's fast pace of modernization appears to be unmatched by the militaries that are likely to deploy alongside the United States in future coalition operations. Such disparity in technological sophistication, it is feared, will lead to coalition incompatibilities, which in turn can undermine the effectiveness of multinational forces. The capability gap caused by differing levels of technological sophistication, coupled with the continuing political need to operate in a multinational environment, may significantly hinder future coalition operations.

The tension between the efficiency of mounting unilateral operations and the political imperative of fielding forces in a coalition setting is well understood conceptually. But as yet there has been little work examining how seriously U.S. Army technological advancements will affect multinational force compatibility (MFC). In light of this, the objective of this study was to determine how—and how significantly—U.S. Army technological developments for Army XXI will influence multinational force compatibility, and to begin exploring what the Army can do to mitigate the effects of such incompatibilities.

The project was undertaken in three parts. First, case studies of recent operations (Gulf War, Haiti, Bosnia) were used to derive MFC lessons learned and to explore how the context of each operation affected the degree of—and need for—coalition compatibility. In the case study analysis, particular attention was paid to how coalitions sought to mitigate technological disparity. The key issues raised by the case studies include the following:

- The technological gap between U.S. and partner forces has been a constant factor in past coalition operations. The impact of technological disparity was not just limited to technical issues; it also shaped operational and political concerns.

- The operational context has played an important role in determining the degree to which such a gap affected coalition performance. Factors such as the intensity of conflict and type of mission, the amount of time to prepare, the extent to which the United States plays a lead role, and the degree of force integration have a great impact on both the amount of MFC achieved and on the need for MFC itself.

- In past operations, mitigation measures (some of which were not necessarily of a high-tech nature) were devised either to eliminate or circumvent the incompatibilities.

Second, comparisons of the U.S. Army's Force XXI modernization process with similar efforts of NATO allies offered a best-case scenario of what technical disparities are likely to appear in the future. This approach assumed that the technological gaps affecting NATO would be even greater in ad hoc operations with non-NATO members. Comparing Force XXI with allied modernization plans leads to the following findings:

- The gap is expected to grow with all partner armies, including the most modern NATO militaries. The disparity lies primarily in the modernization of "software" and command, control, communications, computers, and intelligence (C4I) systems, as opposed to weapon platforms.

- Technological disparity can potentially cause numerous incompatibilities. In a high-intensity conflict that places a premium on speed of maneuver and fast-paced operations against a large and well-entrenched force, nondigitized partner contingents can hinder Army XXI units and undermine the coalition effort. As in the past, however, the magnitude and relevance of the incompatibility will depend on situational factors.

- Indeed, given the evolutionary (rather than revolutionary, as in the case of the Army After Next) nature of the Force XXI process, its development will most likely exacerbate existing incompatibilities with allies and coalition partners rather than create new ones.

Finally, the project team built a framework that characterizes the problems arising from technological disparities and identifies appropriate responses. This allows a systematic analysis of potential MFC problems and solutions. The framework includes the implications of technology gaps (whether technical, operational, or political), the nature of multinational command and control (integrated or separated), the nature of the operation itself (high or low intensity, type of mission, short or long warning), and the range of available mitigation measures. It also discusses how some of the mitigation measures used in the past can be adjusted so that they are applicable in the future. The framework indicates that:

- If the engagement undertaken is a longer-term one, then it is preferable to focus on "fixes" that reduce incompatibility at its roots through such initiatives as combined training and doctrine, multilateral command post exercises, combined research and development, and intelligence-sharing protocols. This is the fastest and most effective route to achieve compatibility among forces with different capabilities.

- When fixes are insufficient or impossible, "workarounds"—efforts to reduce the effects of incompatibilities—remain a viable alternative, allowing forces with different technical capabilities and operating procedures to coordinate their efforts. Although fixes are ideal, workarounds may become increasingly necessary when the technological gap cannot be fixed due to limited resources or because a coalition needs to deploy with little notice.

- The same mitigation measures used in the past should apply in future operations, with some modification to take into account the "digital" nature of future Army XXI units. Army XXI planners need to anticipate and adjust for those requirements that are likely to undermine their efforts at efficiency (e.g., more bloated headquarters, logistical support) and could even affect their operations (e.g., coalition partners' force protection requirements, concerns about fratricide with less-networked contingents, partitioning of the area of operations).

The framework also suggests that engagement efforts will be key. Even as its modernization efforts set the standard for other advanced armies, the U.S. Army's engagement activities can help ensure cooperative and constructive relations with foreign militaries—securing not just technological but also operational and political compatibility over time. The kinds of long-term engagement activities that have underpinned NATO; inspired the American, British, Canadian, and Australian Armies' (ABCA) Standardization Program; and spread U.S. doctrine, equipment, and training worldwide (through International Military Education and Training, Foreign Military Sales, and other security assistance efforts) will be increasingly important. Readiness to deploy liaisons and coalition support teams to bridge gaps and enhance coalition cohesion is crucial.

This challenge also calls for a broader U.S. Army vision. Rather than treating modernization and coalition-building as separate efforts, the Army can combine them as part of a larger strategy.[1] It should establish bureaucratic mechanisms to monitor and evaluate how future

---

[1]This subject will be covered in detail in forthcoming RAND Arroyo Center research by Thomas S. Szayna et al., "Improving Army Planning for Future Multinational Coalition Operations."

modernization programs will affect MFC. The Army should also devise MFC enhancement packages for a number of friendly countries.
Such packages would vary their emphasis on fixes and workarounds,
according to the capabilities of each partner army and the types of
missions to which such forces would contribute .

Efforts to bridge the dual pressures for technological development
and engagement can be pursued within the context of long-term
Army institutional and operational interests. Such an approach can
also help the Army balance its responsibilities and resources in an
environment characterized by a broader array of missions and
increasingly constrained resources.

ACKNOWLEDGMENTS

The authors are grateful to Iris Kameny, Randall Steeb, Sean Edwards, and numerous others both at RAND and in the U.S. Army who took the time to discuss their work and its relevance to the question posed in this study. Brian Nichiporuk was closely involved throughout. Peter Ryan is owed a particular debt of gratitude for his patience and assistance, not the least in providing substantive and constructive criticism and contributions over the course of the study. Paul Davis and Jay Parker reviewed the manuscript and made a number of very valuable suggestions. Any errors are, of course, the authors' own.

AAN	Army After Next
ABCA	American, British, Canadian, and Australian Armies' Standardization Program
ABCS	Army Battle Command System
ARCENT	Army Component, Central Command
ARRC	Allied Command Europe Rapid Reaction Corps
ASAS	All Source Analysis System
ATacCS	Army Tactical Computing System
ATACMS	Army Tactical Missile System
AWE	Advanced warfighting experiment
BCTT	Battle Command Training Team
BMS	Battle management system
C2	Command and control
C2SIP	Command and control systems interoperability program
C3IC	Coalition Coordination, Communication, and Integration Center (Operation Desert Storm)
C4I	Command, control, communications, computers, and intelligence
CARICOM	Caribbean Community

CENTCOM	United States Central Command
COTS	Commercial off-the-shelf
CRONOS	Crisis Response Operations in NATO Operating Systems
CST	Coalition Support Team
DTLOMS	Doctrine, Training, Leader Development, Organization, Materiel, and Soldier
EPLRS	Enhanced position location and reporting system
FBCB2	Force XXI Battle Command–Brigade and Below
FBMS	Formation-level battle management system
FMS	Foreign military sales
FuWES	Fuehrung und Waffen-Einsatz-System
GPS	Global positioning system
HF	High frequency
HUMINT	Human intelligence
IFOR	NATO Implementation Force
IMET	International Military Education and Training
IPB	Intelligence preparation of the battlefield
IPMs	International Police Monitors
JFC	Joint Forces Command (Operation Desert Storm)
JROC	Joint Requirements Council
JSTARS	Joint Surveillance Target Attack Radar System
JTASC	Joint Training Analysis Simulation Center
LN	Lead nation
LNO	Liaison officer
LOCE	Linked Operations Intelligence Centers Europe
MARCENT	Marine Component, Central Command

MEADS	Medium extended air defense system
MLRS	Multiple-launch rocket system
MND	Multinational division
MNF	Multinational Force (Operation Uphold Democracy)
MSE	Mobile subscriber equipment
NATO	North Atlantic Treaty Organization
NORDPOL	Nordic-Polish Brigade
ODS	Operation Desert Storm
OJE	Operation Joint Endeavor
OPCON	Operational control
OPTEMPO	Operating tempo
PfP	Partnership for Peace
SATCOM	Satellite communications
SFOR	NATO Stabilization Force
SHAPE	Supreme Headquarters, Allied Powers Europe
SICF	Systeme d'Information du Commandement des Forces
SID	Simulations Integration Division
SINCGARS	Single Channel Ground and Airborne Radio System
STAGNAG	NATO Standardization Agreement
STU	Secure telephone unit
TACON	Tactical control
TACSAT	Tactical satellite communications
TAV	Total asset visibility
THAAD	Theater high altitude area defense system
TMD	Theater missile defense

TRADOC	U.S. Army Training and Doctrine Command
TTPs	Training, tactics, and procedures
UAV	Unmanned aerial vehicles
UHF	Ultra-high frequency
UNMIH	United Nations Mission in Haiti
UNPROFOR	United Nations Protection Force
USAREUR	United States Army Europe

Chapter One

INTRODUCTION

The U.S. Army, traditionally the least platform-oriented of the U.S. military services, foresees a future in which "boots on the ground" are augmented by a sophisticated command, control, communications, computer, and intelligence (C4I) network, not to mention other new technologies that will endow soldiers with unprecedented speed, precision, situational awareness, and logistical efficiency. Developments toward this future force are being undertaken in two distinct, but complementary, phases. A division of the first phase, Army XXI, is to be in place by the end of 2000, with a corps ready by the end of 2004. The second phase, the Army After Next (AAN),[1] is expected to be operational within the 2020–2025 timeframe.

The Force XXI and AAN processes are elements of the same long-term plan, but they represent different approaches to development. Army XXI will operate current systems enhanced with information age technology. It is rooted in the U.S. Army's AirLand Battle doctrine, and some of its aspects were already fielded in Iraq in 1991. Eventually the entire Army is expected to have Force XXI capabilities.

The AAN, in contrast, will be a revolutionary change and will include organizations and systems that do not yet exist. The AAN is foreseen as a small part of the Army, comprising elite Battle Forces subdivided into Battle Units. These will be the U.S. Army's spearhead: units

---

[1]Just as the term Force XXI refers to the process of developing Army XXI, there is an Army After Next process that is intended to lead to the development of the AAN. This report distinguishes the analysis and evaluation program from the force that is intended to emerge from it by referring, respectively, to the AAN process and the AAN.

capable of rapid deployment, short-term sustainability, and entirely new methods of combat, with Army XXI units forming the more conventional follow-on force.

Yet, political and economic circumstances will militate more than ever against the kind of unilateral operations that can best capitalize on the anticipated Force XXI and AAN developments. Most major wars of this century have been multilateral,[2] and international approbation for the 1989 U.S. operation in Panama signaled a diminished tolerance for unilateral military action even in operations other than war. Such a tendency was mirrored in the angry international response to French unilateral activities in Rwanda in 1994 and has since been borne out by the plethora of multilateral peace, humanitarian, and noncombatant evacuation operations.

There is thus some tension between the pressure for modernization and the need to operate in a coalition environment. Multilateral operations demand a certain level of compatibility, and yet even the United States' closest allies are not modernizing their armies apace with the U.S. Army. U.S. Army units are also just as likely to operate alongside relatively unfamiliar forces as with allied armies, further challenging their ability to achieve compatibility.[3]

This project focused on the concept of multinational force compatibility, or MFC, rather than the narrower concept of interoperability. This approach still recognizes that disparities in technological capabilities can have technological repercussions. For example, at the technical level, technological gaps may yield "mechanical" problems: Can X-nation's gas nozzles fit in Y-nation's gas tanks? Can X-nation's radios communicate with Y-nation's? Can X-nation's computers interface with Y-nation's computers to share information? In an environment where U.S. forces will be relying on digital communication, operating alongside partners with incompatible hardware or software will present difficulties.

---

[2]Steve Bowman, "Historical and Cultural Influences on Coalition Operations," Chapter 1 in Thomas J. Marshall (ed.), with Phillip Kaiser and Job Kessmeier, *Problems and Solutions in Future Coalition Operations*, Carlisle Barracks, PA: Strategic Studies Institute (SSI), U.S. Army War College, December 1997, p. 1.

[3]This does not mean, however, that ad hoc coalition operations will not involve NATO allies. In fact, as argued in this report, European allies are the most likely to participate in high-intensity operations alongside U.S. units.

But the MFC concept also incorporates the notion that technological disparities can have tactical/operational and political effects. If, for example, the United States plans to conduct night operations using its state-of-the-art night-vision equipment, will coalition partners be able to participate? If the United States plans to send small, highly mobile units to use standoff tactics on a nonlinear battlefield, will coalition partners be able to contribute? In the past, the United States has had trouble with non-European coalition partners who were not familiar with air-support operations. There appears to be high potential for problems of this nature to increase as the U.S. Army integrates new technologies.

Finally, in terms of political compatibility, sensitivities are likely to arise in response to very real divergences in capabilities. Is it likely that other nations will allow their troops onto a battlefield where U.S. soldiers—in standoff positions, operating space-based systems, or working in small, highly mobile units with minimal footprints—are nowhere to be seen? How will coalition partners respond to U.S. information dominance? The political questions likely to arise in response to technological developments and related changes in the U.S. Army's tactics should not be discounted or overlooked.

OBJECTIVE

In light of the above considerations, the objective of this study was to examine and weigh the tension between the U.S. Army's rapid technological development and its interests in maintaining or establishing compatibility with foreign armies. Because the AAN remains in the conceptual phase, the project team focused on Force XXI developments. The team sought to determine

- how Force XXI developments are likely to outpace allies' or potential coalition partners' capabilities;

- whether that will inevitably create problems for future combined efforts (and if so, what kind and under what circumstances); and

- whether steps can be taken in the short or long term to avoid, ameliorate, or resolve such problems.

The project had two specific emphases. The first was on compatibility instead of interoperability. The concept of compatibility allows for broader analysis, to include the political and operational implications of technological development as well as the purely technical ones. That said, the project's focus was limited to Force XXI's implications for multilateral operations; political and operational coalition issues were addressed, but only in the context of the U.S. Army's modernization plans. This document seeks to complement more technical analyses by examining the issue of multinational force compatibility and Force XXI in a broader context.

METHODOLOGY

The research was undertaken in three parts. The first task examined past coalition operations[4] to derive lessons for multinational force compatibility. The different operational contexts of Operation Desert Storm in the Persian Gulf, Operation Uphold Democracy and the United Mission in Haiti, and NATO's Implementation Force (IFOR) in Bosnia and Herzegovina offer useful insights into the types of compatibility problems that arose as a result of gaps in technological capabilities. The three case studies also offer insights into how past coalitions sought to eliminate or circumvent incompatibilities among their members.

The project's second task looked forward, assessing how ongoing and anticipated Force XXI developments are likely to stress existing capability disparities between the U.S. Army and its West European counterparts. The assumption underlying this task was that compatibility problems between the United States and its fairly modern and cooperative NATO allies would in all likelihood be exacerbated in any other coalition.

The final task identified ways to deflect, mitigate, or solve anticipated coalition problems stemming from Force XXI developments. The team analyzed the findings from the first and second tasks and developed a framework for conceptualizing, anticipating, and redressing the various capability gaps and resulting compatibility issues that are likely to arise in future coalitions. This framework is

---

[4]Our project refers to multinational operations generically, but it uses the term "alliance operations" specifically in reference to those taking place within the context of NATO or the CFC in South Korea, in keeping with the most recent draft of U.S. Army Field Manual (FM) 100-8, *The Army in Multinational Operations*.

intended to serve as a starting point for Army planners who need to consider how best to prepare for different types of future coalition operations.

OUTLINE

The structure of this report reflects the three project tasks described above. Chapter Two provides a summary of the compatibility issues that emerged in past operations. It is based on a detailed analysis (presented in Appendix A) of the MFC dilemmas that arose in the case study operations. Chapter Three examines the defining features of Force XXI, along with allied efforts at modernizing and digitizing their land forces. It also speculates on problems that are likely to arise as a result of the technological disparity. Chapter Four discusses how incompatibilities were addressed in past operations, then outlines a framework for tackling incompatibilities in future operations.

Chapter Two

COMPATIBILITY ISSUES IN PAST OPERATIONS

In recent years the United States has participated in a number of military operations of varying intensity, involving armies from partner countries with different technological capabilities and operational concepts. While future multinational force compatibility will depend on the specific characteristics of each operation and its participants, the experience gained from past deployments offers important lessons on the types of problems likely to arise and the types of measures that can be employed to address them.

Comparing and contrasting operations Desert Storm in the Persian Gulf, Uphold Democracy and the UN Mission in Haiti (UNMIH), and the NATO Implementation Force (IFOR) in Bosnia made it possible to scan for compatibility issues as they arose in different contexts. We analyzed each operation in terms of the technical, operational, and political problems caused by technological disparities among the coalition members. We gave particular attention to identifying the specific initiatives undertaken to diminish the impact of such disparities. We looked at which compatibility problems (and their solutions) were uniform across the cases, and which were unique to each operation. Identifying patterns across cases made it possible to detect persistent problems, robust solutions, and the impact of situation-specific factors such as intensity of conflict and nature of the coalition. The following is a summary of the case-by-case analysis, which can be found in Appendix A.

COMPARING THE OPERATIONS' BASIC FEATURES

Table 2.1 summarizes the differences and similarities among the three case studies in terms of their basic characteristics, such as the intensity of conflict and type of mission, command and control arrangements, the role played by the United States, and the amount of lead time between the emergence of the crisis and actual deployment.[1]

The operations were different in type and in their command and control arrangements. For instance, the operation in Iraq was a major theater war involving a large counteroffensive, and it was managed with a parallel command structure (albeit with lead-nation overtones). In contrast, the Bosnia effort was an integrated peace enforcement mission that sought to stabilize a war-torn country. The operations were more similar in terms of the role played by the United States, since in all cases American involvement was crucial. The U.S. role was less preponderant in IFOR than in the other two case studies, in part due to the large contribution of other NATO allies. In all the operations, military and political planners had a long time to prepare before execution. Although the several months available for preparation before the operation in Iraq were made

Table 2.1

The Operations Compared

	Intensity and Mission Type	Command and Control	U.S. Role	Timing
Iraq	Major theater war; counteroffensive	Parallel (with lead nation overtones)	Dominant	Long lead time
Haiti	Peacekeeping; stabilization	Lead nation	Dominant	Long lead time
Bosnia	Peace enforcement; stabilization	NATO integrated military structure	Important	Long lead time

---

[1]To be sure, other characteristics can be used to summarize these operations. The case study analysis in Appendix A suggests that the four categories displayed here are particularly helpful in comparing and contrasting the three deployments.

possible by Saddam Hussein's unusual strategy, the timing and pattern of deployment in Haiti and Bosnia were the result of a deliberate decision not to become involved in the conflict until a broad coalition could be structured and deployed in relative safety. To secure a multinational coalition in Haiti, for instance, the United States spent months building support for an intervention force composed of U.S. and non-U.S. forces.

SUMMARIZING THE MAIN COMPATIBILITY CHALLENGES

Some compatibility issues were prominent in all three cases. Often, the root cause of the lack of compatibility derived from technological disparities. Gaps in C4I compatibility were most obviously influenced by technology, but technological issues also shaped differing operating procedures. The Haiti case offers an example of this at the most basic level: Indian military police had insufficient vehicles and radios to undertake independent operations in their areas of responsibility, and required augmentation. At a more sophisticated level, only those forces with night-vision equipment in Iraq could move at the speed of U.S. units and fight according to AirLand precepts. Furthermore, political sensitivities to organizational and operational decisions within the coalitions were often responses to technological disparities. When thinking about the positioning of national contingents on the battlefield and operational command and control, U.S. planners often had to assuage the fears of partners—such as the Saudis during Desert Storm—about U.S. technological dominance.

These basic problems were present in all coalitions examined, but they affected the operations in different ways, as summarized in Table 2.2. As the table's first column implies, the intensity of conflict and type of mission were important factors in determining the impact of incompatibility: In Iraq, compatibility problems were evident and potentially much more serious given the need to drive a large number of Iraqi troops out of Kuwait. In Haiti and Bosnia, where the environment was relatively benign, difficulties in achieving compatibility were less pivotal in determining the success of the operation. To be sure, such incompatibilities could have proved disastrous had the conflict intensified unexpectedly. Moreover, had NATO decided to focus on the capture of war criminals in addition to performing

Table 2.2

General Problems and Responses Across Operations

	Intensity and Mission Type	Command and Control	U.S. Role	Timing
Iraq	High-intensity counteroffensive, greater risk	Parallel/lead-nation C2 eased incompatibility issues	U.S. help key, intelligence problematic	Time to prepare, short war
Haiti	No opposition stabilization force, less strain	U.S./UN problems, but liaison helped	U.S. help key, intelligence problematic	Training, phased deployment helped
Bosnia	Little opposition stabilization	Integrated C2 demanding	U.S. help important, intelligence shared	Training and planning essential, rotation problematic

stabilization missions, the need for compatibility would likely have increased in order to minimize Alliance casualties.

Similarly, one can glance down the command and control column and deduce how increasing levels of integration affected the need for compatibility. The parallel/lead-nation hybrid structure of Desert Storm operations placed fewer strains on multinational command and control by separating forces into different sectors. This had significant military and political benefits: the lead-nation overtone of the C2 structure allowed the United States to centralize the conduct of the operation, placing less strain on coordination. To make the integrated military structure in Bosnia work, it was particularly important to have compatible communications and intelligence capabilities as well as a clear definition of command relationships. C2 problems experienced in Bosnia reflect the fact that achieving full military integration may be difficult, since nations are often unwilling to cede control of their forces to a multinational commander. All things being equal, an integrated command structure in which C2 and operations do not rely extensively on geographic separation demands greater compatibility among the coalition partners. An integrated military structure may only be feasible with fairly modern partners, who share similar operational concepts and have compatible doctrine and C2 procedures.

The ability and willingness of the United States to play a lead role was critical in solving or minimizing some compatibility problems in all operations. In Haiti, the differences in operating procedures between the United States and the UN were at times problematic, but the clear lead role played by the United States in the field of C4I and logistics greatly minimized the relevance of compatibility issues. Simply put, coalition partners in Haiti did not have a C4I system to be made compatible with what the United States deployed. The willingness to share intelligence with coalition partners seems to have increased over time, although the high degree of information sharing in Bosnia was partly related to the alliance nature of the operation.

The chart also underscores the importance of timing. In these operations, lead time was well used to provide common training and exercises, share equipment, and otherwise address potential compatibility problems. Had the United States chosen a quicker response time, most compatibility problems would not have been solved or circumvented before execution, and could have seriously undermined operational effectiveness.

SUMMARY

The analysis of three recent coalition operations suggests that contextual variables affect the nature of the compatibility problems likely to arise in such deployments. The intensity of conflict and type of mission, the command and control structure, the amount of U.S. involvement, and time to prepare are among the key variables. The context of the three past operations under review also provides guidance on what types of mitigation measures are most appropriate in varying conditions. These issues are described in more detail in Chapter Four. The next chapter sets up that discussion by examining the impact that Force XXI and allied modernization efforts are likely to have on future multinational force compatibility.

Chapter Three

LOOKING AHEAD: FORCE XXI AND MULTINATIONAL FORCE COMPATIBILITY

Several defense analysts have expressed concern that U.S. modernization initiatives such as Force XXI will outpace similar efforts by partner countries quickly enough to make effective coalition operations much more difficult.[1] This chapter seeks to contribute to the debate by examining the Force XXI process and the modernization efforts of some of the most competent partners—the NATO allies. We then examine the potential incompatibility problems of fielding Army XXI units alongside the forces of less modern allies.

Analyzing the compatibility issues likely to arise in Army XXI coalition operations is an uncertain endeavor. This reflects the fact that Force XXI concepts are currently undergoing a series of experiments—some of which have highlighted operational problems of digitization[2]—and may be altered before the first digitized division is fielded by the end of the year 2000. Informed speculation is possible, however, especially by taking into account Army XXI's main features and the likely capabilities of allies. Although it is important to

---

[1]See, for instance, David C. Gompert, Richard L. Kugler, Martin C. Libicki, *Mind the Gap*, Washington, D.C.: National University Press, 1999.

[2]According to a 1997 briefing of the Institute for Defense Analyses (IDA), during an early Force XXI large-scale field trial the new C4I system did not produce the expected increases in lethality, survivability, or operational tempo. The average message completion rate was lower than as baseline set by nondigitized troops before the experiment. Overall, the IDA brief concludes that "there was no compelling evidence of increased lethality and survivability, reduced fratricide or increased OPTEMPO relative to the nondigitized baseline brigades." The Logistics Command and Control system also performed below expectations, while the tactical operations centers crucial for C2 functions are not mobile and efficient enough. For instance, see "Questions Raised on AWE Successes," *Defense Week*, October 27, 1997.

recognize that the United States should be prepared to work alongside non-NATO partners, the focus on NATO armies provides a best-case scenario for future MFC.

FUTURE ARMY PLANS AND FORCE XXI

Army XXI is the first stage of the U.S. Army's effort to achieve "full-spectrum dominance" in prompt and sustained joint operations. The Army's broader modernization strategy, which includes both Army XXI and the AAN, is based on *Army Vision 2010* (the Army's support for *Joint Vision 2010*). *Army Vision 2010* defines the operational patterns that, combined with high-quality soldiers and technological advances, are expected to provide essential land-power capabilities to future joint operations. Army XXI is the first step in this process. It absorbs the major equipment such as the Apache Longbow AH64D, M1A1 Abrams, and M2A1 Bradley and seeks to optimize their utility through "digitization," the application of information technologies to acquire, exchange, and employ timely data throughout the operational area.

A key feature of Army XXI is the Army Battle Command System (ABCS), the network of C4I systems that links the Army XXI force. ABCS is a "system of systems" that will provide command and control from the individual soldier up to the theater ground force component commander and beyond. The ABCS will use broadcast battlefield information, including real-time data on friendly and enemy locations as well as information from other sources, to create a graphical depiction of the operation. Army XXI units will no longer rely on the traditional frameworks of battlefield geometry—phase lines, objectives, and battle positions. Instead they will operate on the basis of shared, real-time information about the arrangement of forces on the battlefield.

The tactical interface of ABCS is the Force XXI Battle Command Brigade and Below (FBCB2). FBCB2 gives each soldier the ability to know his or her location, the location of his or her friends, and the location of his or her enemies. Through the graphic interface known as appliqué, FBCB2 provides battlefield information to soldiers by integrating data from GPS and weapons sensors aboard tanks, scout vehicles, and other platforms and from external updates via its digital radio link to an Internet-like data-sharing network. FBCB2 will be found on every platform from the Land Warrior individual soldier system to the Abrams tank.[3]

Digitization is therefore expected to release soldiers from the constraints of traditional military organization, offering instead shared situational awareness and information dominance (superior ability to access and manipulate information). More specifically, Force XXI is intended to achieve operational benefits by

- enabling faster and more precise force-tailoring to avoid intermediate staging and assembly requirements, reduce U.S. forces' vulnerability, and reduce time to combat;

- allowing standoff, nonlinear, dispersed operations through the development of deep precision fire systems such as the Multiple-Launch Rocket System (MLRS) and the Army Tactical Missile System (ATACMS);

- creating superior situational awareness—perhaps the cornerstone of Army XXI—through digitization (of the sort tested at the National Training Center) and the global positioning system (GPS);

- reducing the footprint of U.S. units on the battlefield by operating in a dispersed fashion (as opposed to massing forces) and by relying on defensive electronic warfare systems;

- allowing leaner logistics through Total Asset Visibility (TAV); and

- facilitating split-based operations through advanced telecommunications technologies, thus cutting the costs of deploying support functions such as intelligence nodes, medical specialists, and transportation planners, who can be "beamed in" via telecommunications rather than physically deployed.

Despite its impressive use of new technology, Force XXI is concerned with incremental, evolutionary improvements to the existing Army. Force XXI is rooted in the 1990s Army of Excellence, itself a product

---

[3]ABCS has three major components: Force XXI Battle Command Brigade and Below (FBCB2), the Army Tactical Command and Control System (ATCCS), and the Global Command and Control System—Army (GCCS-A). See *Army Weapon Systems Handbook*, 1999, pp. 2–3.

of AirLand Battle doctrine. Clear precursors of Force XXI developments were present in Operation Desert Storm, from superior situational awareness to high-speed operations, massing of effects, and precision deep fires.

In contrast, the AAN offers the potential for a "revolution in military affairs." The AAN process envisions largely self-deployable air-mechanized raiding units offering strategic reach. The AAN process is expected to innovate both doctrine and force design, not to mention employ revolutionary technology in the areas of vehicle propulsion, logistics, signature control for both ground and aerial vehicles (tilt rotor aircraft and helicopters), and tube weapons.[4] Only a small portion of the Army will be reconfigured for the AAN, acting as a spearhead to shock, stun, and disorient heavier enemy forces until the relatively slower-deploying Army XXI divisions arrive to roll them back and secure victory. The AAN is expected to be in place sometime between 2020 and 2025.

While AAN operations are likely to create radically new MFC requirements, the scope of this analysis is more near term. The following discussion focuses exclusively on the MFC issues likely to arise in Army XXI coalition operations in the next ten to fifteen years.[5]

Force XXI Doctrine and Multinational Operations

Force XXI doctrinal publications highlight the requirement to be compatible with friendly forces in coalition operations. Army doctrine places considerable emphasis on the need to ensure compatibility in the areas of C4I and combat service support (CSS). TRADOC Pamphlet 525-5, *Force XXI Operations*, states as a goal that Force XXI operations are to be conducted under conditions where U.S. forces—

---

[4]For some interesting ideas, see *Summary Report on the Concepts of the Integrated Idea Team (IIT) on Operational and Tactical Mobility,* available at the Training and Doctrine Command's Army After Next Web site: http://www.monroe.army.mil/dcsdoc/aan.htm.

[5]The 4th Infantry Division at Fort Hood, Texas is slated to become the first digitized division by the year 2000. In the FY02 to FY03 timeframe, the 1st Cavalry Division at Fort Hood will become the second digitized unit. The rest of the fully digitized corps, including Army Reserve and National Guard elements, is scheduled to be completed by FY04.

supported by coalition partners—enjoy an information advantage. To fulfill such a vision, TRADOC Pamphlet 525-66, *Operational Capability Requirements*, states that Army battle management systems must be interoperable with those of coalition partners. The pamphlet further claims that Army units will "require total, uninterrupted, interoperable communications between government and nongovernment agencies, and joint and combined forces throughout the battlespace from the National Command Authority to operator level." Moreover, Army XXI units will be expected to "access, leverage and interoperate with multinational organizations and capabilities, as well as to assist in the tracking of friendly forces."[6] Coalition combat service support is discussed in TRADOC Pamphlet 525-53, which states that U.S. "CSS doctrine also must emphasize the joint and multinational nature of CSS operations," including the possibility of executing CSS missions in support of a coalition force.[7]

Aside from the lofty goals for multinational force compatibility, Force XXI doctrine is silent on the issue of what specific problems are likely to arise, and what mitigation measures should be considered. In order to anticipate these, a better understanding of allied modernization efforts is necessary.

WIDENING THE GAP: IMPLICATIONS FOR NATO OPERATIONS

Since the end of the Cold War, most West European militaries have sought to become more modern and acquire new capabilities. They have begun to shift their defense priorities from territorial defense to power projection, developing smaller, more mobile, and more lethal armed forces. This is reflected, as in the United States, by new weapons purchases and an emphasis on digitization.

An assessment of multinational force compatibility must take these advances into account. They may offset the technology gap exacerbated by Force XXI; on the other hand, if the kinds of modernization

---

[6]*Intel XXI—A Concept for Force XXI Intelligence Operations*, TRADOC Pamphlet 525-75, November 1, 1996.

[7]*Operational Concept—Combat Service Support*, TRADOC Pamphlet 525-53, April 1, 1997.

and the concomitant development of doctrine and operational procedures do not coincide with—or actually diverge from—U.S. efforts, compatibility problems may be worsened.

Weapon Systems

A brief examination of current and future weapon system acquisitions by European allies can provide some insight into possible incompatibilities with Army XXI. Drawing upon current and projected capabilities, and taking into account budgetary trends and political constraints, Table 3.1 highlights key allied ground force capabilities that might be relevant to coalitions with NATO allies in the near future. This list is not exhaustive. It does not, for example, set out the all-important weapons with which platforms will have to be equipped. Nor does it go into numbers or address operational quality or professional standards. Its accuracy, furthermore, will depend upon individual countries' own plans over the next few years. Nevertheless, the table offers insights into the relative capabilities of European counterparts.

As the table illustrates, some European allies have in their arsenals key equipment for the conduct of Army XXI operations, such as MLRS and Apache.[8] In other cases, European armies will be able to field counterparts to U.S. systems, as in the case of the Abrams Main Battle Tank, the Paladin,[9] Bradleys, and the Comanche. A number of NATO allies field Patriot systems, some have limited missile defense capabilities, and others will be working with the United States to develop the Medium Extended Air Defense System (MEADS).

A number of European countries have also registered some progress in making these weapon systems more rapidly deployable than in the past. While most NATO allies are only at the beginning of this process, several countries have programs in place to acquire medium- to long-range airlift capability, in the form of C-17s, C-130Js, Antonov An-70s, or the planned Future Large Aircraft. This increased lift

---

[8]Rupert Pengelley, "New British Army Doctrine Makes Apache Chief of All-Arms Battle," *Jane's International Defence Review*, March 1998, p. 5.

[9]The Paladin may eventually be overtaken by the Crusader; however, the future of that system is in doubt.

Table 3.1

Selected U.S./NATO Allied Army Weapon Systems

System	Foreign Military Sales	Foreign Counterparts
Comanche		France/Germany (Tiger)
Apache Longbow	Netherlands U.K.	
Abrams		France (LeClerc) Germany (Leopard 2) Italy (Ariete) U.K. (Challenger 2)
Bradley Fire Support Team Vehicle		France (AMX-10, AMX VTT/LT) U.K. (MCV Warrior MAOV, FV-432AV)
Bradley M2 Infantry/M3 Cavalry Fighting Vehicle		France (AMX-10P, AMX VCI) Germany (Marder 1) U.K. (MCV-80 Warrior, FV-432)
Paladin		France (155 GCT) Germany (PzH 2000) U.K. (AS90)
Multiple Launch Rocket System (MLRS)	Denmark France Germany Greece Italy Netherlands Norway Turkey U.K.	
ATACMS	Turkey (Blocks I/IA)	France (Hades), Blocks I/IA
Patriot[a]	Germany Netherlands	
Joint STARS		France (Horizon) Italy (Creso) U.K. (Astor)
MEADS[b]	Italy/Germany	

SOURCE: U.S. Army, *Weapon Systems, 1997 and 1998.*

NOTE: For a list of programs that deal with interoperability issues, see page 41, footnote 9.

[a]Germany and the Netherlands are currently participating in Patriot acquisition programs.

[b]MEADS is a trinational program between the United States, Germany, and Italy.

capability is extremely important in enhancing compatibility with the United States, since it will allow better synchronization of operations and a more rapid response.

The very existence of the same or comparable European weapon systems, however, does not ensure compatibility with the United States. Such systems may not be connected to command and control systems similar to the ones fielded by Army XXI units,[10] and the doctrine guiding their operations may not be as focused as U.S. doctrine is on maneuver. At the same time, however, similarities between European and U.S. units in terms of the hardware deployed for battle are important. They imply, at the very least, greater potential for technological and doctrinal compatibility. Operations with other coalition partners who do not have similar systems (particularly standoff capabilities) are likely to be more complicated.

Digitization

Where a critical gap *is* emerging between the United States and allied armies is in the digitization process. As mentioned above, digitization underpins Army XXI. Although most NATO allies have sought to enhance their C4I capabilities in recent years, their digitization efforts continue to fall far short of the U.S. Army's. Of the NATO allies, Britain, France, and Germany have embarked on the most comprehensive ground force digitization programs thus far.

The 1996 British digitization strategy calls for the "provision of modern digital command and control functionality to the army's formation headquarters [from division headquarters to theater commander],"[11] the creation of an automated battle management

---

[10]For example, the French and German armies have shelved plans to equip the new-generation Tiger attack helicopter with highly advanced information systems. See "Western Europe Delays Military Digitization," *Defense News*, October 28, 1997.

[11]This formation-level capability (FBMS) is to be based on the existing CIS (IARRCIS) deployed with Allied Command Europe's Rapid Reaction Corps in Germany, and elements of the U.K. Land Command. The revamped Enhanced IARRCIS (also referred to as ATacCS/Army Tactical Computing System) is to enter service next year, providing a client-server architecture and including office automation, messaging facilities, and a geographic information system. See Rupert Pengelley, "International Digitizers Wrestle with Reality," *International Defense Review*, September 1997, pp. 38–46.

system that extends down to the weapon platform and dismounted soldier level, and, eventually, the introduction of Britain's first fully integrated digitized platforms. Other equipment expected to enter service in the short term should also boost British C4I capabilities, including the airborne ground surveillance radar (ASTOR), a battle-field unmanned target acquisition vehicle (PHOENIX), an artillery locating radar (COBRA), and the new generation of battlefield recon-naissance vehicles (TRACER).[12]

France and Germany have also laid out digitization maps. Budgetary restrictions are likely to slow the implementation of such plans, how-ever. The French army did unveil its new formation-level command information system SICF (Systeme d'Information du Commande-ment des Forces) in Bosnia.[13] French land forces are also beginning to develop concepts for digitization at lower levels of command, as in the case of their dismounted-soldier information system demonstrator. French army plans include a three-level battle man-agement system that will be tested by the end of 2000. Following the operational trials, the French will conduct field experimentation of a digital brigade by the end of 2002.[14]

The German army, for its part, is developing its battalion-and-below battle management system (BMS). The system is expected to rely on commercial off-the-shelf (COTS) products and commercial software. Germany will also acquire a command and weapon control system (Fuehrung und Waffen-Einsatz-System, or FuWES). Germany has yet to make provision for appropriate communications systems at plat-form and soldier levels, however—only about 1,000 VHF vehicular radios have so far been ordered, and all are destined for command posts.[15]

Europeans lag further behind in the deployment of smart weapons and automated logistics systems. NATO allies are unlikely to deploy in the foreseeable future long-range and precise fires, such as

---

[12]U.K. Ministry of Defence, *British Strategic Defence Review*, paragraph 148, 1998.

[13]The French army has yet to decide on a platform-level vehicular system to com-plement the SICF. See Pengelley, op. cit.

[14]"French Army Plans Three-Level Strategy," *Jane's Defence Week On-line*, May 6, 1999.

[15]Pengelley, op. cit.

ATACMS (Block II)-like weapons equipped with Brilliant Anti-Tank (BAT) submunitions. The concept of total asset visibility (TAV) and streamlined logistics systems has also received limited attention by European army planners.

Potential Problems

Despite these efforts at digitization, even the most advanced NATO allies have not been able to keep up with the multiple U.S. Army digitization plans. The systems outlined above are not as pervasive, fast, or interconnected as those expected to be fielded by Army XXI units. This is potentially problematic for multinational force compatibility.

The most obvious compatibility problems involve fully digitized units attempting to operate alongside less sophisticated counterparts. The potential effects include compromising and depleting U.S. capabilities (in terms of both combat and combat support), increasing the probability of fratricide, creating unacceptable vulnerabilities among allies or coalition partners, and exacerbating political fault lines in the coalition. Partners with lower operating tempos (OPTEMPOs), lethality, and survivability are more likely to become enemy targets than their Army XXI counterparts. If the United States does not assist with force protection, the viability of the coalition will be threatened politically and operationally. If it does assist with force protection, its own efforts will be slowed and its resources taxed. Similarly, partners with less efficient logistics systems may become targets (if they build up "iron mountains"), requiring U.S. force protection; they may require direct U.S. logistical support; and they may slow the operation.

Incompatible allied units would also be an unexploitable resource for U.S. situational awareness because they would not be able to efficiently report enemy locations and transfer this data into the U.S. tactical Internet. Moreover, partners lacking the level of situational awareness available to U.S. units are likely to be less efficient and effective and even potentially dangerous to the U.S. units if they are not capable of tracking U.S. ground force movements. Such deficits may also lead to U.S. attempts to micromanage coalition partners, with the associated political stresses this may cause.

Fire support coordination and operations in a weapons of mass destruction (WMD) environment will be particularly challenging tasks. Fire support coordination needs to be responsive and backed by highly mobile units with long ranges. The precision of Army XXI fire support will allow such units to assist friendly forces engaged in close combat without a great risk of friendly fire casualties. Standoff fire support from nondigitized units may not be as helpful, since they could not rely on precision weapons and on a real-time picture of battlefield developments. Moreover, Army XXI fire support units may be unable to lay down broad fields of fire if friendly nondigitized forces cannot maneuver quickly enough.[16]

The threat of WMD further exacerbates incompatibilities between Army XXI and nondigitized partner forces. Army XXI units may be able to better withstand WMD attacks by dispersing, moving rapidly, and by detecting the presence of airborne toxins early on. These options may only be partly available to slower, nondigitized units operating in physically concentrated formations. Such units will either have to dig in to prevent heavy losses or continue moving and suffer significant casualties. In the first case, the coalition operation would suffer because entire contingents would be immobilized; in the second, partner casualties could become a significant burden on the coalition.[17]

Problems may also arise in coalitions where all members have reached a comparable level of C4I modernization. Even if coalition partners field digitized forces, they may rely on different hardware and/or software, making them technically incompatible with U.S. systems. The likelihood of this problem arising is enhanced by the rate of technological progress, which has already begun to nullify the concept of fielding standardized equipment across the whole of the U.S. Army, much less among allies or coalition partners. Another issue complicating compatibility between digitized national contingents is network protection. Since digitized units will depend heavily upon information, protecting that information will be paramount, with obvious implications for sharing data among digitized coalition units, especially if some field networks are deemed less secure than

---

[16]Gompert, Kugler, and Libicki, op. cit., p. 35.

[17]Ibid., pp. 35–36.

others. Finally, unless C4I modernization is accompanied by an extension of digitization to individual weapon systems, munitions, and combat service support activities, multinational force compatibility is likely to suffer.

The potential for compatibility problems resulting from digitization is thus great. Indeed, the U.S. Army would face similar challenges if it chose to deploy a hybrid force of Army XXI and nondigitized units in the near future. Ensuring compatibility at the joint level is another challenge. From the standpoint of multinational force compatibility, ongoing U.S. Army efforts to ensure internal and joint compatibility in light of digitization efforts can only be beneficial. Particular care will have to be exercised in ensuring that such procedures could be used with coalition units as well.

SUMMARY

As in the case studies, the importance of the potential problems described above will vary with each situation. The nature of the coalition will have an impact, since establishing operational compatibility will be more difficult in ad hoc coalitions than in alliances. The nature of the conflict and type of mission can also influence MFC, since the difference in performance between Army XXI and other coalition units is probably greatest in a high-intensity, fast-paced major theater war. The level of coalition compatibility will also be determined by the amount of time to prepare, test, and field different systems before deployment.

Indeed, situational factors will determine how much digital interconnection and data sharing is really needed. It seems quite likely that the cost of incompatibilities is much higher if allied commanders cannot speak to one another and get their objectives and rules of engagement straight, than if lower-level officers, much less soldiers, cannot communicate across national boundaries. This is especially the case for lower-intensity operations that will rely on geographic separation to some extent. In high-intensity warfare the requirements are likely to be greater because of the need for layered leak-proof defenses and because, in nonlinear combat, friendly forces might become entangled geographically.

The lessons from the recent Kosovo crisis may prompt European militaries to invest more resources in intelligence-gathering equipment and combat management systems, including digital C4I, space-based assets, and unmanned aerial vehicles (UAVs).[18]   Yet the discrepancy in modernization priorities and budgets between the United States and even its closest allies will increase the likelihood of incompatibilities in any effort. The technology gap that characterized past operations will continue to grow. Overall, it is clear that Force XXI developments will generally exacerbate current coalition problems—technically, operationally, and politically—and will prove more challenging than in the past.

---

[18]See, for instance, J.A.C. Lewis, "Crisis Could Define Future French Spending," *Jane's Defence Weekly On-line*, May 17, 1999.

Chapter Four

MITIGATING THE EFFECTS OF
TECHNOLOGICAL DISPARITIES

To address the incompatibility problems that arose in past coalition operations, U.S. military planners had to devise a variety of mitigation measures. Some were long-term, continuous efforts; others were applied just before or during deployment. This section analyzes the mitigation measures from past operations, considers their relevance in the Army XXI era, and offers a framework to assist U.S. planners in mitigating coalition incompatibility.

LESSONS LEARNED FROM PAST OPERATIONS

The case studies summarized in Chapter Two provided a number of useful lessons for mitigating the technical, operational, and political[1] effects of technological disparities. Table 4.1 lists the various mitigation measures adopted during the three operations. Broad categories of problems arising from technology gaps are presented in the first column. These are separated into (1) C4I, (2) logistics and deployability, and (3) doctrine, procedures, and employment. The second column addresses whether the mitigation measures undertaken were technological, operational, or organizational in nature. The third, fourth, and fifth columns list the mitigation measures employed in each operation.

---

[1]The technological disparities can actually cause problems between national governments participating in the coalition. For instance, political problems may arise when a country wishes its contingent to be assigned a prestigious mission despite its lack of technological sophistication.

Table 4.1

Incompatibility Mitigation Measures, by Problem and Operation

Problems		Iraq	Haiti	Bosnia
C4I	Operational	• C4I liaison	• C4I liaison	• Commercial SATCOM
		• Equipment	• Equipment	• Exercises
		• Training	• Training	
	Organizational	• Geographic separation	• Geographic separation	• Geographic separation
		• C3IC	• Preplanning	• Preplanning
				• Shared systems
	Technological	• Loaned equipment	• Loaned equipment	• Loaned equipment
		• Common equipment (for some allies)	• Some COTS	• Common equipment (for some allies)
				• Joint development
				• COTS

Table 4.1—continued

Problems		Iraq	Haiti	Bosnia
Logistics and Deployability	Operational	• Forecasting coalition needs	• Forecasting coalition needs • Phased deployment	• Forecasting coalition needs
	Organizational	• Geographic separation • Stovepiping	• Geographic separation	• Geographic separation • Stovepiping
	Technological	• Loaned equipment • Common equipment (for some allies)	• Loaned equipment	• Common (some loaned) equipment
Doctrine, Procedures, and Employment	Operational	• Predeployment exercises and predeployment exercises with allies • Liaison	• Predeployment exercises • Liaison	• Predeployment exercises • Regular exercises • Liaison
	Organizational	• Geographic separation	• Geographic separation	• Geographic separation • Common doctrine and procedures
	Technological	• Loaned equipment • Common equipment (for some allies)	• Loaned equipment	• Common (some loaned) equipment

As Table 4.1 illustrates, some mitigation measures were robust across operations, while the employment of others depended on the circumstances of each deployment. For instance, equipment was loaned in all three operations, but only IFOR benefited from common doctrine and procedures.

Some measures were not only adopted across operations, but were also helpful in solving incompatibility problems of different types in each deployment. For instance, geographic separation and loaned equipment were useful in minimizing the effects of technological incompatibility in the areas of C4I, logistics/deployability, and operational concepts. Both measures dampened the harmful effects of incompatibility, either by minimizing contact among contingents or by preventing the use of incompatible equipment. A related enabling factor was the role played by the United States in organizing and conducting each operation. Many mitigation measures were feasible only because of the strong U.S. presence. Across the case studies, virtually all the equipment loans, liaison, and C4I support originated from American forces.

Fixes and Workarounds

A closer look at Table 4.1 suggests a useful distinction. Problems arising from technological incompatibilities may be addressed in two broad ways: either through "fixes" or through "workarounds." "Fixing" a problem involves *reducing incompatibility at its roots* through sharing technology or developing long-term combined policies and planning to bridge technology gaps with nontechnological means. For example, multilateral technology research and development is a fix, as is the development of combined doctrine. "Workarounds," by comparison, seek to *reduce the effects of incompatibilities rather than reducing the incompatibilities themselves.* Geographic separation of incompatible contingents is a workaround widely used in past operations.

Among the mitigation measures that would qualify as fixes are the following:

- **Technological cooperation:** a long-term solution involving cooperative ventures, joint development, standard-setting, and shared research. For alliances, this also involves devising common communications and information systems. By definition, it cannot be undertaken in the face of a crisis.

- **Common equipment:** the joint procurement of the same assets and systems in order to align operational and technological capabilities, as well as to simplify logistics and other support functions. Common equipment can be encouraged through foreign military sales (FMS).

- **Regular training and exercises:** a sustained effort, allowing armed forces to maintain compatibility over an extended period. Such training and exercises can also allow coalition partners to develop capabilities they otherwise would not have had. Programs such as the International Military Education and Training (IMET) program and NATO's Partnership for Peace (PfP) initiative represent examples of this fix.

- **Cooperative doctrine and planning:** coordinated development of operating procedures to ensure consideration of, and compensation for, various partners' capabilities, objectives, and standards. Such efforts also ensure mutual understanding of terminology.

Various workarounds include the following:

- **Geographic separation:** placing national contingents, usually at the division level or above, in sectors, allowing them to operate relatively independently, and thereby avoiding problems of language, operational, and technological compatibility. Integration at the division level or above would make less relevant those compatibility problems that can arise from different support structures and combat equipment.

- **Predeployment planning:** identifying incompatibilities and working with partners to develop an operational concept that minimizes them. Preplanning also involves forecasting coalition needs before deployment and attempting to meet those requirements.

- **Loaned equipment:** a much shorter-term alternative to common equipment, in which the countries with the more sophisticated equipment provide their systems (sometimes with related training) to partners for the duration of an operation.

- **Reliance on commercial, off-the-shelf equipment:** a coalition-wide decision, in the absence of enemy countermeasures, to operate with commercial equipment (such as satellites and radio transmitters) to which all partners have equal access.

- **Phased deployment:** deploying the most capable forces first, then following up with the other contingents once the situation is stabilized.

- **Predeployment training, liaison teams:** more capable partners provide training, equipment and operators, or advice to less capable partners to enhance the latter's ability to conduct more sophisticated operations (thereby preventing an entire coalition from being drawn down to the lowest common denominator).

Workarounds tend to be much cheaper than fixes, can be undertaken much more quickly, and can temporarily address significant problems with relatively little short-term effort. On the other hand, workarounds may create other rifts within the coalition. Geographic separation, for example, can increase the vulnerability of weaker contingents and may be politically unpalatable (if a government is unsatisfied with the placement of its contingent or refuses foreign training). Moreover, workarounds are not usually robust. Loaned equipment must be returned. Phased deployments do not redress the gaps in contingents' capabilities, they simply sidestep the problems such gaps might cause. And, finally, many workarounds may require some lead time, a luxury that will not always be available.

Fixes, in contrast to workarounds, represent real change; they address the roots of compatibility problems. Their effects, therefore, are often long-lasting. But such benefits come at a price. Fixing compatibility problems entails serious political and economic commitments, often over time, as well as a level of trust between nations that may not exist. At times, it simply may not be possible to "fix" some compatibility problems, either because less capable partner countries do not have the capacity, budget, or organization to adopt more advanced technologies or because political and strategic imperatives preclude such cooperation. At other times, when cooperation with a given coalition partner appears to be a singular event, it may not be worthwhile to allocate significant resources to fixes.

Case-by-Case Characteristics

The case studies also demonstrated that the severity of problems created by technological disparities varied with circumstances. Though it is important to recognize the costs and benefits of workarounds and fixes from the "push" side (their inherent qualities), it is equally important to consider their utility and relative value from the "pull" side (based on the specific problems that arise in a given coalition operation). The case studies indicate that the three variables most likely to determine which mitigation measures are appropriate for a given operation include (1) the degree of integration among the forces (whether the coalition is alliance-based or ad hoc),[2] (2) whether the operation in question is high intensity or low intensity,[3] and (3) how much lead time is available before the operation. These variations must be taken into account if mitigation measures are to be calibrated to potential problems. To be sure, these three variables cannot cover the entire spectrum of possibilities. However, they are important contextual factors and can lead to useful generalizations.

Table 4.2 compares the various push and pull factors across two illustrative cases: a long-developing/low-intensity operation undertaken by an ad hoc coalition (assuming a severe capability gap between U.S. and other contingents) and a short-notice/high-intensity alliance operation. The bold text indicates fixes, while the rest of the mitigation measures are workarounds.

The table includes two very different cases for illustrative purposes, and it allows some useful comparisons. For example, it is evident that U.S. provision of C4I capabilities, lift, and logistics remains a useful option in both cases. Yet this is an expensive, and potentially compromising, workaround. A fix useful across both kinds of operations and all three problem areas is the sale of U.S. equipment to

---

[2]Even in ad hoc operations, some coalition partners may achieve a higher level of integration with U.S. forces than others do. For instance, in Desert Storm British and French units were able to benefit from their familiarity with alliance standards and procedures even though the operation was of an ad hoc nature.

[3]The intensity of conflict will change according to the type of mission. All other things being equal, an operation other than war (OOTW) with a peacemaking mission (disarming warring factions, capturing war criminals) has a higher intensity than an OOTW whose mission is to patrol and stabilize a given geographic area.

Table 4.2

Push and Pull Factors in Deriving Mitigation Measures

Problems		Ad Hoc, Low Intensity, Long Lead Time	Alliance, High Intensity, Short Lead Time
C4I	Operational	Provide C4I, liaisons; IMET, predeployment MTTs; **develop intel-sharing protocols**	Provide C4I, liaison; **develop combined exercise training and intel-sharing protocols**
	Organizational	Establish lead-nation C2 structure, geographic separation; set up C3IC	**Integrate C2 structure, forces**; or establish geographic separation
	Technological	Loan/share/**sell** equipment; rely on lowest common denominator, COTS, SATCOM	Loan/share/**sell** equipment; rely on lowest common denominator; **jointly develop equipment**; rely on COTS, SATCOM where not compromised
Logistics and Deployability	Operational	Phase deployment; provide logistics and lift; lease lift, local transportation	**Implement combined total asset visibility (TAV)**; provide logistics and lift; **preposition materiel**; lease local transportation
	Organizational	Establish geographic separation; stovepiping	**Develop combined, complementary lift and logistics planning and structure**; or stovepipe
	Technological	Loan/share/**sell** equipment	**Share, co-develop TAV capabilities; coordinate procurement to ensure compatibility**

Table 4.2—continued

Problems	Ad Hoc, Low Intensity, Long Lead Time	Alliance, High Intensity, Short Lead Time
Doctrine, Procedures, and Employment		
Operational	Provide liaisons; IMET; predeployment MTTs, **standardized and predeployment exercises; invite LNOs to TRADOC, War College, other Army centers**; provide missing capabilities (e.g., force protection); establish a quick reaction force	**Develop combined doctrine, training, exercises, exchanges, etc.**; provide missing capabilities (e.g., force protection); and **compensate in combined planning**
Organizational	Establish lead-nation C2 structure, geographic separation	**Integrate command structure, forces**; partly rely on geographic separation
Technological	Loan/share/**sell** equipment; rely on COTS	Loan/share/**sell** equipment; **co-develop equipment and materiel; establish compatibility protocols**

allies and potential coalition partners. But this may be ruled out as an option by a series of factors, including U.S. national security concerns and potential partners' budgetary constraints. Geographic separation appears to be a fairly robust workaround across all the potential problem areas within both kinds of operations, although it is less desirable than integration since it is less efficient and reinforces fault lines between coalition partners. It would also prove unsuitable in fast-paced, high-intensity conflicts that demand rapid movements across different zones of the battlefield.

There are, of course, intervening combinations of the three variables. In addition to the two cited in the table, it is also possible to have (1) ad hoc low-intensity operations with short lead times, (2) ad hoc high-intensity operations with long lead times, (3) ad hoc high-intensity operations with short lead times, (4) alliance low-intensity operations with long lead times, (5) alliance low-intensity operations with short lead times, and (6) alliance high-intensity operations with long lead times.

The eight possible variations of operations can be reduced into three types for analytical purposes. The degree of integration in a coalition appears to be a key influence on which mitigation efforts will be most feasible and appropriate. This in turn reflects the fact that integration is likely to happen with competent and fairly modern militaries, such as NATO armies.[4] Whether an operation has long or short warning appears to be the second-most influential factor. Although the intensity of an operation will determine how important it is to respond to problems arising from technological disparities, it does not seem to be a critical factor in shaping the appropriate response.

Examining the compressed framework (see Appendix B) facilitates a systematic analysis of the complex interactions between types of

- problems arising from technology gaps;
- coalition operations; and
- mitigation measures.

---

[4]If the United States wanted to establish integrated operations with countries outside established alliances (such as Saudi Arabia), it would have to face a very difficult set of compatibility challenges.

Arguably, the most challenging problems will arise in short-term high-intensity operations, in which forces are closely integrated. The high level of integration may be desired either because the operation is being undertaken by an alliance such as NATO, or because geographic separation is deemed to be ineffective. These problems can best be addressed with fixes, which by their nature are easiest to implement within alliances. In this case the framework would prescribe a set of NATO-style initiatives on joint doctrinal development, technology sharing, and other forms of cooperation. Failures to coordinate and cooperate in preparation for such conflicts (whether as a result of parochial industrial interests or national security concerns) will be costly, since workarounds are unlikely to suffice. In contrast, even though some fixes, such as international military education and training (IMET) and foreign military sales (FMS), will help prepare the United States and potential partners to operate in ad hoc coalitions, workarounds will probably remain necessary.[5] Though not ideal, workarounds have proved sufficient in past low-intensity operations, especially when there was time before deployment to conduct combined exercises and training, develop operational protocols, and define an acceptable C2 structure.

More generally, the framework helps to set priorities by suggesting which mitigation measures apply to more than one type of problem and/or to more than one type of operation, and by identifying which are most crucial (those that enable a strong multinational response to high-intensity short-warning operations). It indicates the value of engagement and long-term preparation for coalition operations. It also makes clear which workarounds are likely to be necessary, suggesting that ready-to-apply protocols and procedures can yield great benefits immediately before and during deployment. Although the framework could be pulled off the shelf to help guide operational planners when a contingency is imminent, it is better applied as a longer-term planning tool for guiding engagement efforts (fixes, in effect) and preparing U.S. military leaders in the likely event workarounds are necessary in future multilateral operations.

---

[5]IMET is funded at extremely low levels, limiting the amount of military-to-military interaction possible. Moreover, foreign military sales are declining substantially and are influenced by political and domestic economic decisions that limit their utility as coalition-strengthening mechanisms.

APPLICATION OF MITIGATION MEASURES IN THE FORCE XXI ERA

As discussed in Chapter Three, the types of coalition problems likely to arise from technological incompatibilities in the Army XXI era will differ more in degree than in type from those encountered in the past. Although many of the mitigation measures that worked in the past will remain relevant for at least the next 15 years, the widening technological gap will require a different balance of such measures.

What will be different? Within the NATO alliance, most key weapons capabilities will be roughly compatible. That will not be the case with most countries' armies, however. In ad hoc coalitions involving less sophisticated national contingents, the United States will need to find ways to mitigate the substantial gaps in mobility, standoff and precision strike capabilities, and force protection.

Digitization will cause more serious compatibility problems in both alliance and ad hoc coalition operations, affecting every aspect of a deployment. The disparity in capabilities will be great enough so that equipment sharing or loans will not be viable options unless there is ample time before an operation to train foreign forces on sophisticated technologies. Selling equipment may also prove problematic in several cases, either because of U.S. national security concerns or because of prohibitive costs. Geographic separation, a steadfast workaround from past operations, may no longer be possible on the nonlinear and fast-changing battlefields of digitized warfare. Longer-term fixes such as the development of combined technologies may become more difficult than in the past, given the sheer complexity (and cost) of new systems. With the rapid advancement of technology, maintaining compatibility across hardware and software will be a persistent challenge.

Some mitigation measure variants could include

- loaned C4I equipment and "digitization" liaisons;
- tagging nondigitized units;
- mission separation;
- allowing interface with less sophisticated C4I systems;

- technological cooperation;

- common equipment;

- regular training with Army XXI units; and

- gaming and simulation to identify and respond to potential problems.

The first four are workarounds; the latter four are fixes. As discussed below, even workarounds may require long-term planning in the Army XXI era.

Loaned C4I Equipment and "Digitization Liaisons"

Although Force XXI experimentation has not specifically addressed the compatibility problems of coalition warfare, it has considered workarounds to improve the battlefield coordination of units with varying levels of digitization. For instance, during the recent Division XXI Advanced Warfighting Experiment (AWE) at the National Training Center, liaison teams proved essential for sharing command and control information when more digitized information transfers were impossible. Liaison teams also served as bridges between adjacent nondigitized units. Other possible solutions include providing C2 systems to selected units joining the digitized force.[6]

Using "digitization liaisons" and loaning C4I equipment are workarounds similar to those employed to mitigate past incompatibility problems. In principle, therefore, they should be applicable not only to nondigitized U.S. forces, but also to nondigitized coalition partner forces. These workarounds require far more technology—which will have to be provided by the United States—than in previous cases.[7] Furthermore, in the case of equipment loans, coalition partners may be able to operate complex U.S. battle man-

---

[6]Specifically, the Army could provide appliqué/Force XXI Battle Command—Brigade and Below (FBCB2) systems to selected units.

[7]It has been estimated that in a digitized unit the liaison officer would require a vehicle with 2x FM radios, tactical satellite communications (TACSAT), mobile subscriber equipment (MSE), enhanced position location and reporting system (EPLRS), and the Force XXI Battle Command—Brigade and Below (FBCB2) command and control system in order to be effective.

agement systems only after extensive training. This implies that, where feasible, the level of preplanning necessary for using liaisons and loaning equipment to allies should be greater than in the past.

Tagging and C4I "Backdoors"

Not all workarounds have to entail complex solutions, however. Two relatively simple mitigation measures would consist of retaining a lowest common denominator capability to ensure that nondigitized or digitized formations running on earlier technology can communicate with the most sophisticated digitized units (such an effort might be termed the use of "analog backdoors"). This solution has already been recognized by U.S. military planners and is likely to be implemented in the future. The second relatively simple solution would consist of electronically tagging nondigitized coalition units in order to monitor their movement on the battlespace. One could augment this approach by adding sensors to allied equipment. The sensors' data output would be processed by U.S. C4I systems. Such a workaround would allow U.S. troops to have a more complete picture, although it would not increase the situational awareness of coalition partners.

Mission Separation

As stated before, a strategy of parceling zones to U.S. and partner forces based on their different capabilities can be problematic in Army XXI operations. Unlike traditional battlefields, terms such as center and flanks may become blurred in fast-paced Army XXI deployments. As the battle becomes deeper, separate operations from different starting points will merge and share the same geographic space.[8]

In the Army XXI era, assuming nonlinear, standoff operations, geographic separation may be less appropriate than mission separation. The U.S. Army, for example, will be ideally suited to deep, offensive battlefield operations. Other coalition members with slower forces and less technologically advanced communications systems might

---

[8]Gompert, Kugler, and Libicki, op. cit., p. 37.

more appropriately take on offensive urban area missions or assume defensive or stability and support responsibilities. Although mission separation will be vulnerable to the same kinds of political sensitivities as geographic separation, it will allow each coalition member to contribute at its own level and would be a realistic response to capabilities gaps. This approach would also enable the more capable partners, such as NATO allies, to be involved in more challenging missions, perhaps alongside U.S. forces. Mission separation and geographic separation may become identical tasks in operations where the battlefield is static, such as in a peacekeeping and stabilization mission.

Technological Cooperation

The United States has already devised programs to foster technological cooperation, especially with NATO allies.[9] Efforts in the field of C4I harmonization, as laid out in the Army's International Digitization Strategy, should be expanded and refined to cover key coalition C4I capabilities.[10] Another example of high-leverage technological cooperation is the recently signed agreement on coalition artillery support. The United States, Great Britain, France, and Germany

---

[9]These include the C4I agencies of NATO's Military Committee, the C4I-related groups under NATO's Conference of National Armaments Directors, the Army Tactical Command and Control Information Systems (ATCCIS) under SHAPE, the Quadrilateral Armies Communications Information Systems Interoperability Group (QACISIG), Artillery Systems Cooperation Activities (ASCA), the Low-Level Air Picture Interface (LLAPI), the ABCA working group on C4I, the C4I Defense Data Exchange Program (DDEP), the Multinational Interoperability Program (MIP), and regular C4I staff talks. The Theater Commanders-in-Chief (CINCs) also regularly plan C4I exercises and engagement efforts with theater allies. See *Tactical Coalition Interoperability*, ADO Briefing, March 16, 1999. Available on the Internet at *http://www.ado.army.mil/Br&doc/TIC/TCI/index.htm.*

[10]According to a recent Army Digitization Office (ADO) briefing on coalition command and control, the shared C4I capabilities of a coalition should include seamless communication across all systems, dynamic network management, friendly and opposing force location updates, asset availability, real-time engagement planning/replanning, "ruggedized" hardware integrated well into battlefield systems, and improved protection from information warfare. *Tactical Coalition Interoperability*, ADO Briefing, March 16, 1999. Available on the Internet at *http://www.ado.army.mil/Br&doc/TIC/ TCI/index.htm.*

have agreed to develop interfaces to each other's artillery support C2 systems, with Italy soon to follow.[11]

Perhaps the most comprehensive technological cooperation effort that Army planners should consider is NATO's Defense Capabilities Initiative (DCI), unveiled at the NATO Washington Summit in April 1999.[12] DCI seeks to improve technological and industrial collaboration within NATO by focusing on key systems and capabilities, such as precision-guided munitions, C4I interoperability, transport assets, airborne ground surveillance systems, and integrated logistics. Within the context of DCI, NATO will establish a multinational logistics agency and devise a new alliance-wide C4I network by 2002.[13] DCI's focus on logistics is warranted, since compatible C4I alone cannot ensure that coalition forces will be as maneuverable and sustainable as their Army XXI counterparts.

Common Equipment

Technological cooperation can also lead to common C4I solutions and weapon systems. Other programs such as foreign military sales can provide key allies with equipment that will make their participation in an Army XXI coalition more compatible (e.g., deep fires).[14]

---

[11]"U.S.-NATO Allies Ink Artillery C2 Cooperation Plan," *C4I News*, Vol. 6, No. 6, April 8, 1999.

[12]DCI represents the culmination of a debate on NATO standardization that took shape in the 1970s. For more background on 1970s analyses of NATO standardization, see "Nobody Wants Standardized Weapons," *Business Week*, May 16, 1977; John L. Clarke, "NATO Standardization: Panacea or Plague?" *Military Review*, April 1979; and Robert Facer, *The Alliance and Europe, Part III: Weapons Procurement in Europe— Capabilities and Choices*, Adelphi Paper Number 108, Winter 1974/75.

[13]Vago Muradian, "NATO Leaders to Unveil Defense Cooperation Effort," *Defense News*, April 26, 1999.

[14]The Assistant Secretary of the Army (Acquisition, Logistics, and Technology) as well as the International Programs division of the Army Materiel Command (AMC) are currently coordinating the development and acquisition of common equipment. Relevant activities include technology exchange and co-development of equipment, systems, and components. The aim is to introduce shared or at least compatible standards in a number of areas, including information exchanges, integrated force management, and employment of precision forces.

Long-Term Training and Planning

Army XXI makes the requirement of training and planning more important than ever, since several Force XXI concepts are still being developed and their impact on coalition operations has yet to be explored. The United States could take advantage of its current cooperation structures, such as IMET and NATO, to encourage training between Army XXI units and counterparts from other countries. The U.S. Army should continue to plan for coalition command post exercises and advanced warfighting experiments (probably at a smaller scale for cost considerations) with key allies, in order to identify problem areas and solutions. Force XXI–specific long-term planning and training should also be useful in reconciling Army XXI doctrine with the operational concepts of partner forces.

Gaming and Simulation

Gaming and simulation should be particularly useful in identifying the requirements for workarounds and fixes, as well as the optimal balance between these two mitigation approaches. These techniques have been embraced at the joint level; for instance, *Joint Vision 2010* argues that

> simulations must be interconnected globally—creating a near-real-time interactive simulation superhighway between our forces in every theater. Each CINC must be able to tap into this global network and connect forces worldwide that would be available for theater operations.

Moreover, the U.S. Atlantic Command intends, ultimately, to establish a system enabling anyone with C4ISR equipment to be able to "plug and play in Distributed Joint Training activities."[15] Such modeling and simulation can help planners anticipate and adjust for incompatibility-related problems in coalitions as well. NATO is the primary candidate for hosting coalition warfare simulations, given the relatively high technological sophistication of its members. At

---

[15]Steve Moore, "The U.S. Atlantic Command Modeling and Simulation Issues," Joint Training Analysis and Simulation Center (JTASC), U.S. Atlantic Command, 2 June 1998.

the same time, the United States needs to involve less sophisticated friendly armies in its gaming activities, since not all U.S. Army operations will be undertaken exclusively with NATO allies.

DTLOMS IMPLICATIONS

Doctrine

Coalition requirements and Force XXI have thus far been dealt with separately in doctrine. Although some of the Force XXI documents refer to the need to ensure interoperability, they do not explicitly guide such efforts. Likewise, doctrine addressing the MFC requirements—such as Field Manual 100-8, *The Army in Multinational Operations*—focuses on issues likely to be relevant immediately before and during a multinational operation. Future doctrine should address these gaps by highlighting the potential operational problems of Army XXI coalition operations. Such doctrinal discussions should also incorporate those measures that can be undertaken to mitigate incompatibility problems, both long before and immediately prior to deployment.

Training

As mentioned above, continued and, in some cases, increased combined training and IMET activities will improve military-to-military familiarity, allowing planners to identify and prepare for or eliminate capability gaps. Such efforts should also include standardized joint and combined simulations and modeling.

Leader Development

Army leaders should be trained and educated to balance the benefits of Force XXI developments against the requirements of coalition operations across the spectrum of conflict. Army leaders will need to understand under what circumstances technology gaps will lead to serious technical, operational, and strategic problems. The use of the framework outlined above should help leaders conceptualize and respond effectively to the tension between Force XXI priorities and coalition demands.

Organization

At the broadest level, existing alliances and organized engagement activities (such as NATO's Partnership for Peace) will remain important means for ensuring compatibility even in the face of technological disparities. Within the U.S. military, the Joint Training Analysis and Simulation Center (JTASC) should be enhanced or augmented to allow more focused attention to the requirements of multinational force operations. Similarly, the U.S. Army's Simulations Integration Division (SID), advanced warfighting experiments, and Battle Command Training Teams (BCTTs) should test and train for Army XXI participation in coalition operations. The U.S. Army should continue to plan for a series of multinational exercises involving Army XXI technology, including a remote command post exercise in 2000, a centralized command post exercise in 2001–2002, and a multinational AWE in 2004.[16]

Materiel

Coalition requirements should help guide how and how much materiel is procured. Quantities considered adequate in a lean, unilateral Army XXI operation, for example, are unlikely to be sufficient in a multinational context. Some slack may have to be built into plans for multinational operations in order to support liaisons and/or shared equipment. Additionally, backdoor technologies to facilitate C4I and logistics coordination among technologically incompatible coalition partners should be available to provide a lowest common denominator capability.

FINAL OBSERVATIONS: TOWARD A BROADER MFC STRATEGY

The framework developed in light of the case study findings will continue to be useful in the Army XXI era, as will the more general lessons concerning the desirability of fixes and workarounds, the requirements for engagement, and the need to anticipate future coalition requirements. The U.S. Army could pay a high price for

---

[16]*Tactical Coalition Interoperability*, Army Digitization Office Briefing, March 16, 1999.

underestimating and failing to prepare for the coalition compatibility problems caused or exacerbated by Force XXI developments. For a future operating environment in which

- the United States cannot afford to operate consistently alone;

- there is a need to hedge against short-warning conflicts, and to promote early intervention;

- variations in capability can create vulnerabilities within a coalition; and

- differences in objectives or rules of engagement can cause the disintegration of coalition efforts or a strategic loss

it will be increasingly important to conduct long-term multilateral planning, research and development, and procurement so as to best ensure future coalitions' compatibility and/or complementarity. This suggests a requirement for continued, if not increased, military-to-military engagement in conjunction with the U.S. Army's technological and doctrinal evolution.

Indeed, in many respects, the U.S. Army is in a historically strong position from which to influence both its own future and that of the broader international security environment. As its modernization efforts set the standards to which other advanced armies will aspire, its engagement efforts can help ensure cooperative and constructive relations with foreign militaries—relations that will help ensure not only technological but also operational and political compatibility over time. With the potential for short-warning contingencies and the need for a rapid response, the types of long-term engagement activities that have underpinned NATO, inspired the American, British, Canadian, and Australian Armies' Standardization Program (ABCA), and spread U.S. doctrine, equipment, and training worldwide (through IMET, FMS, and other security assistance efforts) will be increasingly important. There may simply be no time to organize last-minute training or protocol development in future coalition operations.

One of the key conclusions from this study is that the optimal combination of mitigation measures depends on the context of each operation. Army planners should develop a comprehensive MFC enhancement strategy that takes into account the compatibility needs of the different operational categories identified in the framework. For instance, standard workaround packages (consisting of liaisons and loaned equipment) should be devised for ad hoc, low-intensity operations. Tailored MFC plans, with varying emphasis on workarounds and fixes, should be formulated for those countries most likely to contribute to critical, high-intensity conflicts. Elaborating on the specifics of these MFC enhancement packages is beyond the scope of this report, and will be addressed in future research. What is important, however, is that Army planners adopt a systematic approach to MFC enhancement that relies on a mix of ad hoc and long-term activities.

This challenge calls for a broader U.S. Army vision. Rather than treating modernization and coalition-building as separate efforts, the Army can combine them as part of a larger strategy. Bridging the dual pressures for technological development and engagement can be done within the context of long-term Army institutional and operational interests. Such an approach can also help the Army balance its responsibilities and resources in an environment characterized by a broader array of missions and increasingly constrained resources.

CASE STUDIES

The cases were selected because they represent diverse kinds of operations, from peace support efforts to major theater war. They also differ in other key characteristics, including coalition structure (parallel, lead-nation, and integrated)[1] and participation, the role played by the United States, and time-related issues such as preparation and duration of operation.

In examining the three operations, particular care was taken to identify which technological disparities were important at what stage, and what was done or could have been done to minimize problems. As previously mentioned, the emphasis of the case studies is on the broader issue of compatibility rather than the narrower, technology-specific question of interoperability.

OPERATION DESERT STORM

Desert Storm was a major theater war that involved over 300,000 U.S. Army troops (at its peak) and 160,000 troops from partner countries.[2] The operation sought to repel the Iraqi invasion of Kuwait as well as destroy Iraq's military capability to wage war. Large force contributions were made by the United Kingdom, France, Saudi

---

[1]See *The Army in Multinational Operations* (FM-100-8), Chapter 2.

[2]The U.S. Marine Corps also participated in the ground component of Desert Storm, with a peak contribution of over 92,000 troops. See Anthony H. Cordesman and Abraham R. Wagner, *The Lessons of Modern War, Volume IV: The Gulf War*, Boulder, CO: Westview Press, 1996, p. 141.

Arabia, Egypt, Syria, Kuwait, and Gulf Cooperation Council (GCC) states.[3]

Command and control arrangements took the form of a U.S.–Saudi Arabia parallel command structure. The American chain of command coordinated the activities of units from the United States and other NATO allies, including the British and French divisions. Most U.S. Army units were part of Army Component, Central Command (ARCENT). ARCENT consisted of the XVIII Airborne Corps and VII Corps; the British division participated in VII Corps's offensive, which constituted the main armored thrust of the ground war. The French division operated in the western flank with XVIII Airborne Corps. Saudi-led forces were organized in Joint Forces Command North and East (JFC-N and JFC-E). JFC-N consisted of Egyptian, Syrian, Saudi, and Kuwaiti forces. It was deployed east of VII Corps. JFC-E occupied the right flank along the coast, and was made up of units from Saudi Arabia and Gulf Cooperation Council states.[4]

The Coalition Coordination, Communication, and Integration Center (C3IC) served as the link between the two chains of command. It facilitated coalition-wide planning, training, firing exercises, logistics, radio frequency management, intelligence gathering and sharing, boundary changes, and fire support.[5] While no coalition member relinquished ultimate control over its military forces, the United States was given substantial freedom to organize and direct the operation. The dominance displayed by the United States in planning, fighting, and supporting Desert Storm effectively made what for-

---

[3]The United Kingdom contributed the 1st Armoured Division, while France sent the 6th French Light Armored Division. Saudi Arabia's forces included five independent brigades and smaller units, while Egypt contributed the 4th Armored Division, 3rd Mechanized Division, and 20th Special Forces Regiment. Syria's 9th Armored Division and Special Forces regiment participated as reserves, and Kuwaiti forces included three independent brigades and smaller units. GCC states Bahrain, Oman, and Qatar also contributed forces. Countries such as Morocco, Canada, Senegal, Pakistan, Hungary, Czechoslovakia, Poland, and Argentina also contributed troops. See Department of Defense, *Conduct of the Persian Gulf War: Final Report to Congress*, April 1992, p. 500; Cordesman and Wagner, op. cit., p. 95.

[4]For a summary of task organization of U.S. and non-U.S. ground forces, see *Conduct of the Persian Gulf War*, op. cit., pp. 232–234 and pp. 257–258.

[5]*Conduct of the Persian Gulf War*, op. cit., pp. 235, 559.

mally was a parallel C2 structure a *de facto* parallel/lead-nation hybrid.

Compatibility Issues

Before and during the ground campaign, several compatibility issues arose in the realm of C4I, doctrine, and procedures. The high-intensity nature of the operation highlighted the presence of several technological and operational incompatibilities among allies. The most U.S.-compatible coalition members were Britain and France, partly because these NATO allies deployed units with previous training in high-intensity operations that placed a premium on maneuver. British and French assets were successfully employed by American C4I systems (SATCOM capability from Britain's SKYNET system, and reconnaissance data from French helicopter-mounted radar).[6] The British armored division integrated with U.S. forces more deeply than its French counterpart did—although the French division was effective in carrying out its mission, it was thought to be too light to engage the best Iraqi units. Due in part to their separation from NATO's military structure, French forces had not exercised with U.S. units intensively enough to be able to use American battle management systems. The lack of night-vision equipment in most French vehicles impeded their full employment at night or under unfavorable weather conditions.[7] The French division also lacked the trained intelligence personnel to adequately carry out the intelligence preparation of the battlefield (IPB) process.[8]

Intelligence sharing was at times problematic. While officers from Britain were well integrated into CENTCOM intelligence operations, the flow of intelligence data among all partners was hampered by U.S. procedures stressing information security. The release of classified information to coalition members was hampered by the lack of clear guidelines and procedures.[9]

---

[6]Cordesman and Wagner, op. cit., pp. 258, 318.

[7]Ibid., pp. 170, 592–599.

[8]James J. Cooke, *100 Miles from Baghdad: With the French in Desert Storm*, Westport, CT: Praeger, 1993, pp. 57–58.

[9]Cordesman and Wagner, op. cit., pp. 281, 289.

Non-NATO coalition partners were less compatible than French and British units; for instance, the C4I systems deployed by Arab partners were not sophisticated and had to be supplemented with U.S. equipment. Arab coalition members were also not prepared—from an organizational and training standpoint—to fight a maneuver war with the high combat tempos characteristic of AirLand Battle. Equipment diversity in Arab arsenals (with systems of varying ages originating from different countries) was a source of logistics problems, since it placed great pressure on spares and maintenance.[10]

Incompatibility Mitigation Measures

While the high intensity of the conflict stressed compatibility among coalition partners, command and control arrangements helped attenuate political and military incompatibility. The existence of a parallel command structure eased Saudi concerns about being part of a U.S.-dominated coalition, and designating Arab forces as part of the Saudi chain of command resolved other political dilemmas, including the impact of Syria's differences with the rest of the coalition (the Syrian division remained in reserve as part of JFC-N). Separation of forces simplified the division of labor and eased compatibility concerns from the technological, operational, and political standpoints. The lead-nation overtones of the parallel C2 structure also facilitated coordination by striking a balance between the need to address political sensitivities and the military requirement to centralize command and control.

Coalition military planners acknowledged the differences in British and French compatibility with U.S. forces, positioning British units with VII Corps in the main thrust of the armored assault and moving the French division to what was thought to be a less demanding sector to the west, alongside forces from the XVIII Airborne Corps.[11] The French *Daguet* Division was clearly separated from the rest of XVIII Corps by using an Iraqi highway (MSR TEXAS) as the boundary

---

[10]For a detailed account of the military shortfalls of non-NATO coalition partners, refer to Cordesman and Wagner, op. cit., pp. 173–209.

[11]*Conduct of the Persian Gulf War*, op. cit., p. 557.

between U.S. and French ground units.[12] Although more compatible than French forces, the British division suffered from important limitations compared with U.S. counterparts. Lack of self-sufficiency in logistics and service support, electronic warfare, and command and control systems was addressed by the provision of U.S. systems and assistance.[13]

The United States also played a key role in loaning equipment to allies. Five ground-mobile force/defense satellite communications systems were transferred to British units to address C2 shortfalls between Britain's command headquarters and British forces on the ground. The United States improved the robustness of Saudi command and control assets by providing secure communications systems such as radios, phones, encryption equipment for computers, and fax machines.[14]

The United States made extensive use of liaison teams to train Saudi forces and to augment their command and control assets. Liaison teams—referred to as non-U.S. Coalition Partner Support Units— were assigned to coalition forces at every command level down to the battalion. Partner Support Units used U.S. communications systems to maintain voice connectivity with U.S. headquarters.[15] Teams of 35 liaison officers were assigned to JFC-North and JFC-East; in addition to providing satellite communications, they operated as battle staff members.[16] Saudi officers have argued that pre-Desert Storm training (under Operation Desert Shield) enhanced their ability to breach the Iraqi forward defenses. U.S. partner support units boosted Saudi communications compatibility with U.S. commands immediately before and during the ground offensive. Moreover,

---

[12]See *The Army in Multinational Operations* (FM-100-8), p. 4-13. Additionally, the U.S. 2nd Brigade, 82nd Airborne Division, and its adjacent French units, the 3rd Rima and the 4th Dragoons, conducted detailed coordination on their respective maneuver plans following the map exercises.

[13]Cordesman and Wagner, op. cit., pp. 143, 158–162.

[14]For instance, in the summer of 1990 Saudi forces acquired more than 100 secure high-frequency (HF) radios. See *Conduct of the Persian Gulf War*, op. cit., pp. 562–568.

[15]Ibid., p. 501.

[16]Cordesman and Wagner, op. cit., p. 561.

U.S.-augmented systems proved to be the most reliable C2 systems for Saudi forces.[17]

There was also considerable use of liaisons between XVIII Airborne Corps and the French division. Corps headquarters, the 82nd Airborne Division, the 24th Infantry Division, the 101st Air Assault Division, and the 18th Field Artillery Brigade exchanged liaison teams with the *Daguet* Division. These teams used organic U.S. radio equipment between the French division headquarters and their parent unit's headquarters. The teams also served as sources of information on the doctrine, tactics, standard operating procedures, force structure, and capabilities of their respective units. To ensure accurate and timely indirect fire during the operation, a U.S. Army fire control system (TACFIRE) detachment was integrated into the French fire support coordination center at *Daguet* Division headquarters to orchestrate fire coordination measures. This ensured face-to-face coordination between U.S. and French artillerymen at the decisionmaking point.[18]

Despite the fast-paced and high-intensity nature of the conflict— which placed a great deal of stress on the performance of coalition members who were neither trained nor equipped to operate in such conditions—the United States was able to mitigate technological disparities by assuming responsibility for most coalition capabilities. For example, the United States provided most coalition C4I. Intelligence collection relied extensively on U.S. satellite systems, while approximately nine-tenths of all airborne coverage originated from U.S. communications and dissemination capabilities.[19] Indeed, the U.S. C4I advantages helped centralize effective command of the operation.

The long lead time between coalition unit deployment in theater and the start of the ground offensive was also important. It allowed friendly forces to improve their combined warfighting effectiveness, making possible, for instance, the substantial Saudi-U.S. training ef-

---

[17]Ibid., p. 183.

[18]Adapted from *The Army in Multinational Operations (FM-100-8)*, p. 2-21.

[19]Cordesman and Wagner, op. cit., p. 282.

fort begun in September 1990.[20] It also allowed the modification of tactical communications systems deployed by the United States, Britain, and France to ensure interoperability.[21] The variety of equipment and standards employed by coalition forces posed unique challenges for the construction of a communication architecture and logistics channels. Such systems had to be improvised, and they required several "workarounds" that became possible only with months of preparation. These short-term compatibility shortcuts may not have functioned appropriately in a higher-intensity, longer conflict, and could have jeopardized operational success.

OPERATION UPHOLD DEMOCRACY AND UNMIH

The peacekeeping and humanitarian assistance nature of Operation Uphold Democracy made the coalition effort, which was centered mainly around ground forces, significantly different from Desert Storm. There were two distinct phases to the multinational operation, with different C2 arrangements. Operation Uphold Democracy was conducted by a U.S.-led multinational force (MNF) deployed in September 1994 to secure domestic law and order. In March 1995, Uphold Democracy and the MNF were followed by a United Nations peacekeeping operation named UNMIH (United Nations Mission in Haiti). UNMIH's mission was to maintain order and promote the democratization of Haiti.

The United States played a preponderant role in both Haiti operations; although U.S. forces substantially decreased from the MNF's peak of 20,000, America was the largest troop contributor to the much smaller UNMIH operation (2,400 out of a total of 6,000 personnel).[22] The lead-nation nature of the coalition allowed the United States to exercise tactical control over all multinational forces. While the MNF/UNMIH transition required adjustment of procedures and systems to reflect the new UN orientation, the United States retained control of the force.

---

[20]Ibid., p. 185.

[21]Ibid., p. 260.

[22]Adam B. Siegel, *The Intervasion of Haiti*, Alexandria, VA: Center for Naval Analyses, Professional Paper 539, August 1996, p. 29.

A large number of countries participated in the Haiti peace operations. The Caribbean Community (CARICOM) and Bangladeshi battalions provided important force contributions in the early phases of MNF and in UNMIH. Troops from other countries, including Pakistan, Nepal, and Canada, widened the multinational element over time.[23] In both operations, participating nations' forces were separated geographically—contingents operated in sectors where they were under the mission commander's control. A quick-reaction force composed of U.S. troops was created to support the separated contingents in crises.[24]

The phasing out of MNF and its replacement with UNMIH allowed coalition forces to deploy in and out of theater at staggered times. While the U.S. military provided almost all of the intervention forces at the outset, the foreign element of Operation Uphold Democracy and UNMIH steadily increased over time. The first non-U.S. contingent to join the MNF was a 266-man composite battalion from CARICOM in early October, followed by the lead element of the Bangladeshi battalion later that month. Smaller Guatemalan and Costa Rican contingents deployed before the end of 1994. The first contingent of International Police Monitors (IPMs) also arrived early in October.[25]

Compatibility Issues

The relatively peaceful nature of the operations and the benign environment encountered by the multinational forces greatly eased the compatibility concerns caused by technological disparity. Overall, command and control arrangements worked well. While the organizational structure of the MNF was subjected to several changes to integrate contingents arriving in theater at different times, no significant stresses were placed on multinational command and control.

The transition from MNF to UNMIH was relatively smooth, although U.S. forces had to adjust to UN procedures and doctrine. Several of

---

[23]For a detailed description of Operation Uphold Democracy, see Siegel, op. cit.

[24]Hal Klepak, "Haiti Takes Its Next Step," *Jane's Defence Weekly*, May 13, 1995, pp. 19–20.

[25]Siegel, op. cit., p. 26.

the lessons learned from Somalia, including the need for a clear chain of command and sufficient time to transfer responsibilities, were applied in the context of UNMIH. The transition from MNF to UNMIH was facilitated by appointing a U.S. commander, by training UN personnel in the United States before the handoff, and by seeking to complete the integration of UNMIH contingents not in MNF well before the official transfer of authority.[26]

The standard UN procedures for C4I and support activities were inconsistent and underdeveloped, and could have led to greater compatibility problems without an active U.S. role. Compatibility concerns arose in the area of communications under UNMIH. Communications was a UN responsibility, and all units to the battalion level were to be provided with telephone service and ultra high frequency (UHF) radio communications to ensure connectivity with UNMIH headquarters. The fact that the UN communications network was not entirely operational immediately after the MNF/UNMIH transfer of authority forced the coalition to rely on a patchwork system that included the Haitian telephone system, two UN INMARSAT terminals, the UHF radio system, U.S. Army tactical satellite terminals, and the U.S.-contracted commercial voice network. The ad hoc nature of the communications system made it vulnerable and did not allow the exchange of classified or encrypted messages among coalition members. UN communications doctrine did not foresee the provision of horizontal communications links between national contingents to complement the vertical ties between the contingents and headquarters. Such communications shortfalls could have made coordination among adjacent but separate forces more problematic in a crisis.[27]

Communications problems extended to the contingent of IPMs, which lacked compatible communication equipment and had only a few vehicles to allow mobility independently of the United States. Some international police units operated under doctrines that were at variance with U.S. military police tactics and procedures. For instance, the Indian police company replacing the U.S. 58th Military

---

[26]Center for Army Lessons Learned, *Operation Uphold Democracy: Initial Impressions*, Volume III (The U.S. Army and United Nations Peacekeeping), July 1995, p. 89.

[27]Ibid., pp. 86–87, 100–101.

Police Company after the transition from MNF to UNMIH had fewer personnel than the 58th and was organized into large, squad-like units. They lacked vehicles for transportation and patrolling, and the few radios they carried were not compatible with U.S. tactical radios. Though well trained and disciplined, the Indian company could not carry out independent operations.[28]

The breadth and sophistication of the C4I systems used by U.S. troops and commanders could not be matched by other participants. In fact, there was no other coalition C4I structure with which to make the U.S. system compatible. U.S. intelligence "releasability" procedures were followed so strictly that almost no intelligence data were directly available to multinational contingents. These procedures were adapted over time, and some information such as imagery was downgraded and released.[29] While most intelligence-sharing issues affected both MNF and UNMIH, some affected only the latter since they were related to differences in U.S. and UN intelligence-gathering doctrines. In UN peacekeeping operations, intelligence activities are usually kept at a minimum and are termed "information operations." The distinctions led to some confusion—at times U.S. military intelligence personnel assumed "UN restricted" information to be equivalent to "U.S. secret." Such confusion stifled the flow of intelligence data, especially in the first months of UNMIH.[30]

Logistics under UNMIH also required adjustments from the United States, since a number of U.S. requests for materiel had to be approved by a UN-appointed Chief Administrative Officer. The UN approval process was often unresponsive and caused delays in the support chain. Despite the presence of a UN logistics framework, the United States remained the chief provider of logistics support for coalition contingents during UNMIH.[31]

---

[28]Ibid., pp. 118–121.

[29]*Operation Uphold Democracy: Joint After Action Report (Draft)*, p. 41, and *Operation Uphold Democracy: Initial Impressions*, Volume II, p. 171.

[30]*Operation Uphold Democracy: Initial Impressions*, Volume III, p. 44.

[31]Ibid., p. 169.

Incompatibility Mitigation Measures

Given the inability of most partners to field their own national support and C4I structures, mission effectiveness hinged on a strong U.S. role. In fact, the United States provided the bulk of communications equipment and logistics support during MNF and UNMIH. American tactical communications systems supported coalition operations, including UN personnel, the CARICOM battalion, the International Police Monitoring Agency, and other coalition forces. Equipment sharing was complemented by the extensive use of liaison teams for C4I support and training.[32] The use of liaisons for intelligence data sharing, for instance, minimized the impact of U.S. doctrinal obstacles to releasing classified information.[33]

A large portion of coalition communication and training support came in the form of coalition support teams (CSTs). Composed of special forces units, CSTs served as advisory groups. CST-supported initiatives included training on American C2 relationships, communications, staff relationships, supply requisitions, and medical procedures. CSTs operated the telecommunications equipment (tactical network phones, SATCOM, SINCGARS) necessary to maintain connectivity between headquarters and the coalition partners. U.S. forces in Haiti supported the CARICOM contingent in other ways, including housing, food, transportation, and vehicle maintenance.[34]

Predeployment training of coalition forces played a crucial role in minimizing compatibility problems—as in the case of the CARICOM battalion. Command and control of the CARICOM battalion was undermined by discipline problems during the Haiti operations, in part due to the battalion commander's lack of authority over troops from different countries. However, the performance of the CARICOM battalion would have worsened considerably without the assistance of the CST prior to and during deployment. The CST joined the CARI-

---

[32]Atlantic Command, *Operation Uphold Democracy: Joint After Action Report (Draft)*, 1995, p. 9.

[33]*Operation Uphold Democracy: Joint After Action Report (Draft)*, p. 41, and *Operation Uphold Democracy: Initial Impressions*, Volume II, p. 171.

[34]Center for Army Lessons Learned, *Operation Uphold Democracy: Initial Impressions*, Volume II (D–20 to D+150), April 1995, pp. 136–138, and *Operation Uphold Democracy: Joint After Action Report (Draft)*, p. 33.

COM battalion in Puerto Rico before MNF and trained CARICOM forces. The close involvement of CST members in CARICOM's training process led to a cooperative relationship between CARICOM and U.S. troops.[35] Troops from Bangladesh as well as IPMs and UN officials also benefited from predeployment training.

Not all potential compatibility issues were addressed by training, however, and not all could be. For instance, the CST trained the CARICOM battalion in basic infantry skills and placed less emphasis on battle staff procedures. In the case of the Indian military police company, incompatibility was caused by different doctrinal requirements and could not be rectified in a short period. Despite its limitations, predeployment training and the use of liaisons helped to bring about a minimum level of compatibility between coalition forces.

The success of the efforts in Haiti is also related to the extensive preparation time available to military planners; in fact, Atlantic Command foresaw the possible use of XVIII Airborne Corps in a forcible entry mission as early as October 1993. The operational plan that guided the deployment of U.S. troops in Haiti was adopted in early September 1994, but it was based on alternative operational plans devised months in advance. The importance of giving Uphold Democracy a multinational character was also foreseen in the planning phase. The United States managed to gain the support of Latin American and Caribbean countries for the operation—leading to the direct involvement of CARICOM and Latin American troops.[36]

Other time-related issues were important in Haiti. The staggered deployment schedule for multinational forces minimized the impact on the operation's conduct of disparities in capabilities and assets among coalition partners. The United States began the MNF phase unilaterally, and other contingents deployed only after U.S. forces could guarantee relative safety. The phased-in deployment also made the preparation and incorporation of less technologically capable units smoother and more manageable. Thus, the timing decisions in Operation Uphold Democracy stemmed from deliberate

---

[35]*Operation Uphold Democracy: Initial Impressions*, Volume II, p. 138.

[36]Siegel, op. cit., p. 9.

efforts to minimize the impact of technological and operational disparities on coalition effectiveness.

NATO'S IMPLEMENTATION FORCE (IFOR)

The NATO Implementation Force (IFOR) was very different from its UN-led peacekeeping predecessor, the United Nations Protection Force (UNPROFOR). IFOR was an alliance operation, with a corps-sized land component composed of the Allied Command Europe Rapid Reaction Corps (ARRC). Its peace enforcement mandate included ensuring compliance by the former warring factions with the cease-fire, maintaining the separation of forces, and ensuring the demobilization of remaining forces.

IFOR had a unified command and was NATO-led, under the political direction and control of the Alliance's North Atlantic Council. Overall military authority was in the hands of NATO's Supreme Allied Commander, Europe (SACEUR), General George Joulwan. General Joulwan designated Admiral Leighton Smith (NATO's Commander in Chief Southern Command (CINCSOUTH)) as the first commander-in-theater of IFOR (COMIFOR). With the retirement of Admiral Smith in July 1996, Admiral Joseph Lopez was appointed as CINC-SOUTH and also replaced Admiral Smith as COMIFOR. For the duration of the Bosnia operation, the COMIFOR headquarters was split-based between Sarajevo and Naples.[37]

Forces were both multinationally integrated and geographically separated. While the three most important contributors—the United States, France, and Britain—operated in different sectors, each led a multinational division (MND) with a considerable number of troops from different countries. The U.S.-led MND, for instance, included brigades from Turkey, Russia, and a third non-U.S. brigade made up of troops from Finland, Sweden, Norway, and Poland (the NORDPOL brigade).

The U.S. role in IFOR was substantial. Its division was the largest, and its deployable satellite communications capabilities proved

---

[37]Larry K. Wentz, "Bosnia—Setting the Stage," in Wentz (ed.), *Lessons from Bosnia: The IFOR Experience*, Washington, D.C.: NDU Press, 1998.

critical in supporting IFOR C4I. The American intelligence effort included manned and unmanned airborne systems, as well as surface
and satellite intelligence platforms. Despite the important role
played by the United States, American superiority was less over-
whelming than in Desert Storm.[38] NATO allies such as Britain,
France, Italy, and Germany deployed their tactical communications
systems, and some communication deficiencies were offset by relying on commercially available assets. Some C4I needs were addressed by alliance-wide information systems. NATO deployed its
own data communications and intelligence sharing systems—Crisis
Response Operations in NATO Operating Systems (CRONOS) and
the Linked Operational Intelligence Centers Europe (LOCE).[39]

European countries were more effective than U.S. forces in collecting
human intelligence (HUMINT), in part due to the links established
by their units during the UNPROFOR operation. U.S. doctrinal requirements also placed restrictions on the ability of American forces
to mix with the local population and collect HUMINT. While signal
intelligence and overhead surveillance were essential, HUMINT
proved to be equally important.[40] Moreover, U.S. high-technology
intelligence assets did not always perform as expected. The Joint
Surveillance Target Attack Radar System (JSTARS), for instance, was
at times unable to distinguish friend from foe given the lack of a clear
dividing line between friendly forces and those of the former warring
parties.[41]

Compatibility Issues

IFOR forces encountered a relatively benign environment. The low
degree of opposition placed minimal stress on the compatibility of
systems and multinational C2 arrangements. The ad hoc C4I system
worked reasonably well, although it was a patchwork of NATO, UN,
national, and commercial systems. Moreover, the NATO analog

[38]Gompert, Kugler, and Libicki, op. cit.

[39]These were not extended to Partnership for Peace (PfP) partners. See Barbara Starr, "Learning Zone," *Jane's Defence Weekly*, May 27, 1998.

[40]*Operation Joint Endeavor Lessons Learned*, U.S. Army Europe, 1996.

[41]Larry K. Wentz, "Intelligence Operations," in Wentz (ed.), op. cit.

interface to ensure system interoperability (STANAG 5040) was slow and did not cover the strategic-tactical integration of voice networks. The ad hoc and patchwork nature of the system caused the C4I architecture to be bloated—given the presence of multiple networks, up to seven different telephone sets could be found at headquarters in the early phases of the operation. Switching calls from one voice network to another was complicated, and calls experienced a 20 percent probability of being blocked in IFOR's early months.[42] The complex and ad hoc nature of NATO's communication and information system also made it vulnerable, although there were no attacks on command facilities and communications infrastructures.[43]

Command and control relationships were at times strained given the differences between SHAPE and IFOR and between the ARRC and the multinational divisions. The command relationships between NATO, IFOR, and USAREUR were at times ill defined. U.S. requirements for force protection and support prompted U.S. Army Europe to deploy a forward headquarters in Hungary, which influenced the operations of the U.S. MND outside IFOR C2.[44] The presence of a relatively large number of forces outside coalition command and control would have become problematic had the conflict unexpectedly intensified.

Some of the compatibility problems in Bosnia reflected NATO's inexperience in forward-deploying significant strategic C4I capabilities. The alliance had no doctrine or operating procedures to guide the planning and implementation of the multinational communications system and intelligence architecture. CRONOS was essential in connecting SHAPE and NATO headquarters with IFOR, but its lack of an interface to national networks meant that data had to be transferred manually from the NATO to national systems. LOCE promoted the sharing of classified information; however, it lacked the

---

[42]David C. Gompert, Richard L. Kugler, and Martin C. Libicki, *Mind the Gap*, Washington, D.C.: National University Press, 1999.

[43]C4I Integration Support Activity (CISA), *Compendium of Operation Joint Endeavor Lessons Learned Activities*, 1996, Chapter 6.

[44]For instance, "force protection teams" were deployed by USAREUR in Bosnia, outside the established NATO command and control structure. See *Bosnia-Herzegovina After Action Report I*, Peacekeeping Institute, Army War College, Carlisle Barracks, PA, 1996.

necessary bandwidth for fast and high-volume communications. Moreover, the United States did not use LOCE to transmit its highly classified information.[45]

Incompatibility Mitigation Measures

Incompatibility and its deleterious impact were decreased before the operation by good planning and training within the Alliance. Military commanders had years to plan for the deployment of their forces, and such lead time allowed Partnership for Peace (PfP) and NATO countries to train prior to deployment. NATO allies also ran several tests to verify the interoperability of their communications equipment.[46]

Nonmilitary communications systems were used and allowed NATO to offset some of the limitations of its C4I structure. The presence of a UN satellite telephone network (a remnant of UNPROFOR) facilitated communications in a mountainous environment. Commercial satellite communications systems provided connectivity between troops on the ground and national and NATO command authorities. However, the rotation of the ARRC out of theater after the transfer of authority from IFOR to SFOR created some difficulties, since the information systems replacing ARRC's were not as functional.[47]

IFOR participants shared intelligence internally to an unprecedented degree and managed to exploit the large contribution of U.S. assets and systems to coalition C4I. In fact, the United States released classified information to allies more quickly and regularly than in Haiti or Desert Storm. NATO devised a new classification category (IFOR-releasable) to maximize the intelligence flow to non-NATO countries. The United States also allowed Russian units to use All Source Analysis System (ASAS) WARLORD intelligence work-

---

[45]Barbara Starr, "Learning Zone," *Jane's Defence Weekly*, May 27, 1998.

[46]Prior to deployment, NATO held a major interoperability exercise (INTEROP 95) to improve system integration and address interface compatibility issues. INTEROP 95, held in April 1995, included more than 250 participants from 8 nations and tested all anticipated interfaces necessary to execute the AFSOUTH and ARRC OPLANs. See Wentz, "C4ISR Systems and Services," in Wentz (ed.), op. cit.

[47]Ibid. On the use of commercial satellites to support strategic connectivity, see also 5th Signal Command, *Operation Joint Endeavor: Lessons Learned Book*, 1997.

stations.[48] While the integration of PfP countries in Bosnia was successful, some of their contingents faced equipment shortages. To address such problems, the United States provided liaison officers and equipment, including STU-IIBs (secure telephone units).[49]

Despite its complexity, the Bosnia operation did not present challenging conditions from a military standpoint. The operation was facilitated by the relative proximity between the theater of operations and NATO territory, making logistics and movement relatively simple. Deployment was also eased by the fact that two framework nations—France and Britain—had troops deployed in theater before the transfer of authority from UNPROFOR to IFOR. Moreover, the security environment in Bosnia remained benign, and the Alliance had several months to plan for the operation and solve several interoperability problems before deployment.

---

[48]However, allies did not always match U.S. openness in sharing information, often adopting strict need-to-know criteria. See Wentz, "Intelligence Operations" and "C4ISR Systems and Services," op. cit.

[49]These efforts, however, were undermined by the fact that a fraction of U.S. forces operated STU-IIIs not interoperable with the NATO standard STU-IIB. PfP contingents also experienced communication problems because of the lack of English speakers among their ranks. See Jeffrey Simon, "The IFOR/SFOR Experience: Lessons Learned by PfP Partners," *Strategic Forum*, Number 120, Institute For Strategic Studies, July 1997, and *Operation Joint Endeavor Lessons Learned*, U.S. Army Europe, 1996.

FRAMEWORK FOR DERIVING MITIGATION MEASURES

See following pages

		(Fixes in Bold)
Problems		Ad Hoc, High or Low Intensity, Long Lead Time
C4I	Operational	Provide C4I, liaisons; **IMET**; predeployment MTTs; **develop intel-sharing protocols**
	Organizational	Establish lead-nation C2 structure, geographic separation; set up C3IC
	Technological	Loan/share/**sell** equipment; rely on lowest common denominator (LDC), COTS, SATCOM where not compromised
Logistics and Deployability	Operational	Phase deployment; provide logistics & lift; **preposition materiel**; lease lift, local transportation
	Organizational	Establish geographic separation; stovepiping
	Technological	Loan/share/**sell** equipment
Doctrine, Procedures, and Employment	Operational	Provide liaisons; **IMET**; predeployment MTTs, **standardized** and predeployment exercises; **invite LNOs to TRADOC, War College, other Army centers**; provide missing capabilities (force protection); establish a quick-reaction force
	Organizational	Establish lead-nation C2 structure, geographic separation
	Technological	Loan/share/**sell** equipment; rely on COTS

(Fixes in Bold)

Ad Hoc, High or Low Intensity, Short Lead Time[a]	Alliance, High or Low Intensity, Long or Short Lead Time
Provide C4I, liaisons; **develop intel-sharing protocols**	Provide C4I, liaison; **develop combined exercise training and intel-sharing protocols**
Establish lead-nation C2 structure, geographic separation; set up C3IC	**Integrate C2 structure, forces**; partly rely on geographic separation
Loan/share/**sell** equipment; rely on LDC, COTS, SATCOM where not compromised	Loan/share/**sell** equipment; rely on LDC, **jointly develop equipment**; rely on COTS, SATCOM where not compromised
Phase deployment; provide logistics & lift; **preposition materiel**; lease local transportation	**Implement combined total asset visibility (TAV); provide logistics & lift; preposition materiel**; lease lift (if long lead time), local transport.
Establish geographic separation; stovepiping	**Develop combined, complementary lift and logistics procedures**; or stovepipe
Loan/share/**sell** equipment	**Share, co-develop TAV; coordinate procurement to ensure compatibility**
Provide liaisons; **IMET; standardized exercises; invite LNOs to TRADOC, War College, other Army centers**; provide missing capabilities (force protection); establish a quick-reaction force	**Develop combined doctrine, training, exercises, exchanges, etc.**; provide missing capabilities (force protection); **and compensate in combined planning**
Establish lead-nation C2 structure, geographic separation	**Integrate command structure, forces**; partly rely on geographic separation
Loan/share/**sell** equipment; rely on COTS	Loan/share/**sell** equipment; **co-develop equipment and materiel; establish compatibility protocols**

[a]The relative importance of fixes and workarounds changes with the amount of lead time: with short lead times, fixes become more important since some workarounds may not be feasible.

Bosnia-Herzegovina After Action Report I, Carlisle Barracks, PA: U.S. Army Peacekeeping Institute, U.S. Army War College, 1996.

Bowman, Steve, "Historical and Cultural Influences on Coalition Operations," in Thomas J. Marshall (ed.), with Phillip Kaiser and Job Kessmeier, *Problems and Solutions in Future Coalition Operations*, Carlisle Barracks, PA: Strategic Studies Institute (SSI), U.S. Army War College, December 1997.

Clarke, John L., "NATO Standardization: Panacea or Plague?" *Military Review*, April 1979.

Compendium of Operation Joint Endeavor Lessons Learned Activities, Washington, D.C.: C4I Integration Support Activity (CISA), Department of Defense, 1996.

Conduct of the Persian Gulf War: Final Report to Congress, Washington, D.C.: Department of Defense, April 1992.

Cooke, James J., *100 Miles from Baghdad: With the French in Desert Storm*, Westport, CT: Praeger, 1993.

Cordesman, Anthony H., and Abraham R. Wagner, *The Lessons of Modern War, Volume IV: The Gulf War*, Boulder, CO: Westview Press, 1996.

Facer, Robert, *The Alliance and Europe, Part III: Weapons Procurement in Europe—Capabilities and Choices*, London: IISS, Adelphi Paper Number 108, Winter 1974/75.

5th Signal Command, *Operation Joint Endeavor: Lessons Learned Book*, 1997.

Gompert, David C., Richard L. Kugler, and Martin C. Libicki, *Mind the Gap*, Washington, D.C.: National University Press, 1999.

Klepak, Hal, "Haiti Takes Its Next Step," *Jane's Defence Weekly*, May 13, 1995, pp. 19–20.

Lewis, J. A. C., "Crisis Could Define Future French Spending," *Jane's Defence Weekly On-line*, May 17, 1999.

Marshall, Thomas J. (ed.), with Phillip Kaiser and Job Kessmeier, *Problems and Solutions in Future Coalition Operations*, Carlisle Barracks, PA: Strategic Studies Institute (SSI), U.S. Army War College, December 1997.

Metz, Steven, "The Effect of Technological Asymmetry on Coalition Operations," in Thomas J. Marshall (ed.), with Phillip Kaiser and Job Kessmeier, *Problems and Solutions in Future Coalition Operations*, Carlisle Barracks, PA: Strategic Studies Institute (SSI), U.S. Army War College, December 1997.

Muradian, Vago, "NATO Leaders to Unveil Defense Cooperation Effort," *Defense News*, April 26, 1999.

"Nobody Wants Standardized Weapons," *Business Week*, May 16, 1977.

Operation Joint Endeavor Lessons Learned, U.S. Army Europe, 1996.

Operation Uphold Democracy: Initial Impressions, Volume II (D–20 to D+150), Fort Leavenworth, KS: Center for Army Lessons Learned, April 1995.

Operation Uphold Democracy: Initial Impressions, Volume III, Carlisle Barracks, PA: Center for Army Lessons Learned, U.S. Army and United Nations Peacekeeping, July 1995.

Operation Uphold Democracy: Joint After Action Report (Draft), U.S. Atlantic Command, 1995.

Pengelley, Rupert, "International Digitizers Wrestle with Reality," *Jane's International Defense Review*, September 1997, pp. 38–46.

———, "New British Army Doctrine Makes Apache Chief of All-Arms Battle," *Jane's International Defense Review*, March 1998, p. 5.

Scales, Robert H., Jr., "Trust, Not Technology, Sustains Coalitions," *Parameters*, Winter 1998–99, pp. 4–10.

Siegel, Adam B., *The Intervasion of Haiti*, Alexandria, VA: Center for Naval Analyses, Professional Paper 539, August 1996.

Simon, Jeffrey, "The IFOR/SFOR Experience: Lessons Learned by PfP Partners", *Strategic Forum*, Number 120, Institute for Strategic Studies, July 1997.

Starr, Barbara, "Learning Zone," *Jane's Defence Weekly*, May 27, 1998.

Summary Report on the Concepts of the Integrated Idea Team (IIT) on Operational and Tactical Mobility, U.S. Army Training and Doctrine Command, http://www.monroe.army.mil/dcsdoc/aan.htm.

The Army in Multinational Operations, U.S. Army Field Manual (FM) 100-8, 1998.

U.K. Ministry of Defence, *British Strategic Defence Review*, 1998.

U.S. Army, *Report to Congress on the Plan for Fielding the First Digitized Division and First Digitized Corps*, 5 August 1998.

Wentz, Larry (ed.), *Lessons from Bosnia: The IFOR Experience*, Washington, D.C.: NDU Press, 1998.